ZENDOODLE COLORING BOOK

COLORING PAGES FOR THE YOUNG AT HEART

Reduce stress and relax with over 60 unique designs

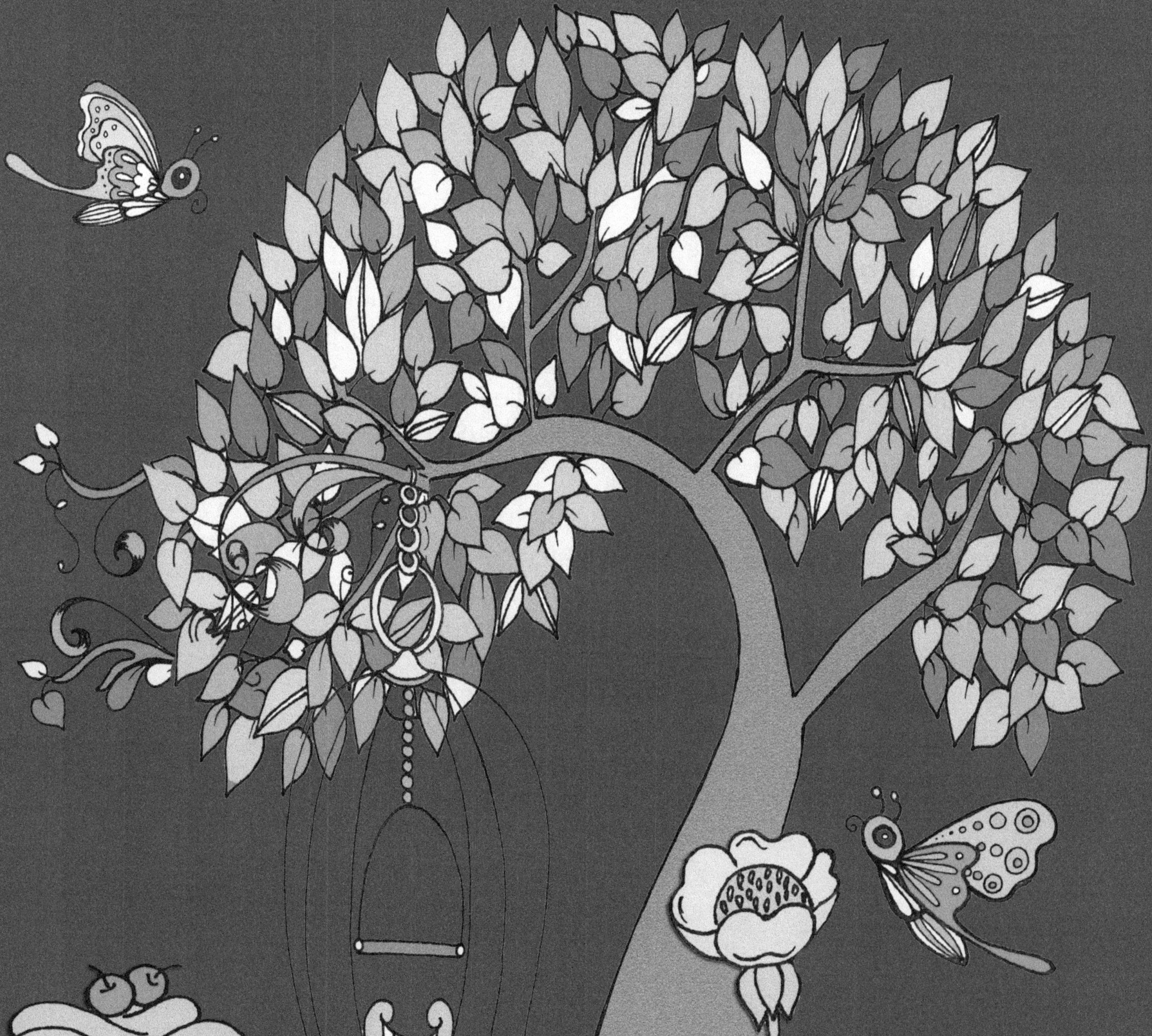

MISTY MCDIVITT

Hillbilly Art
5333 Fort Henry Drive
Kingsport, TN 37663
www.facebook.com/hillbillyartcoloringbooks
hillbillyart77@outlook.com

Printed in the United States of America

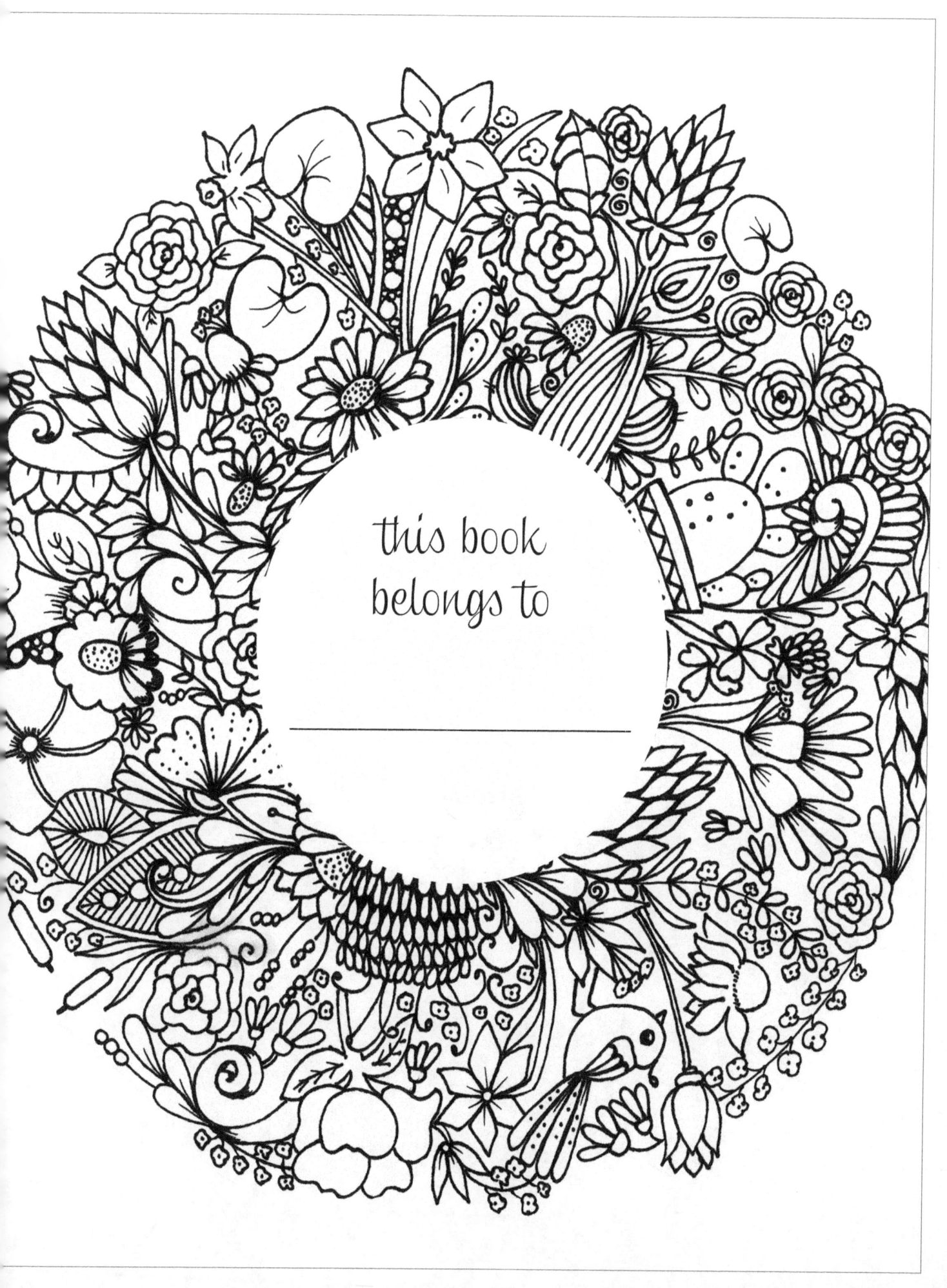

this book
belongs to

_____

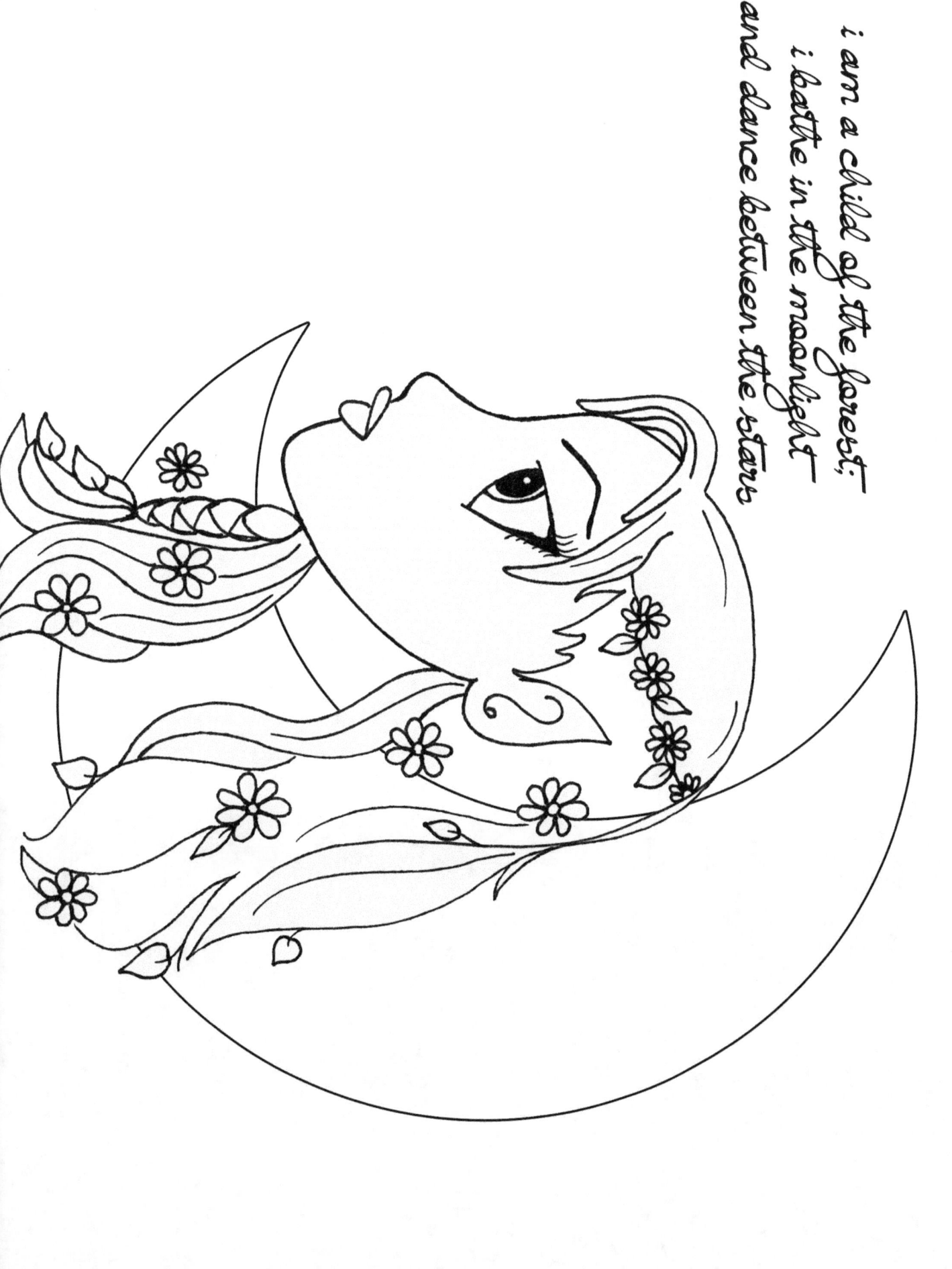

i am a child of the forest;
i bathe in the moonlight
and dance between the stars

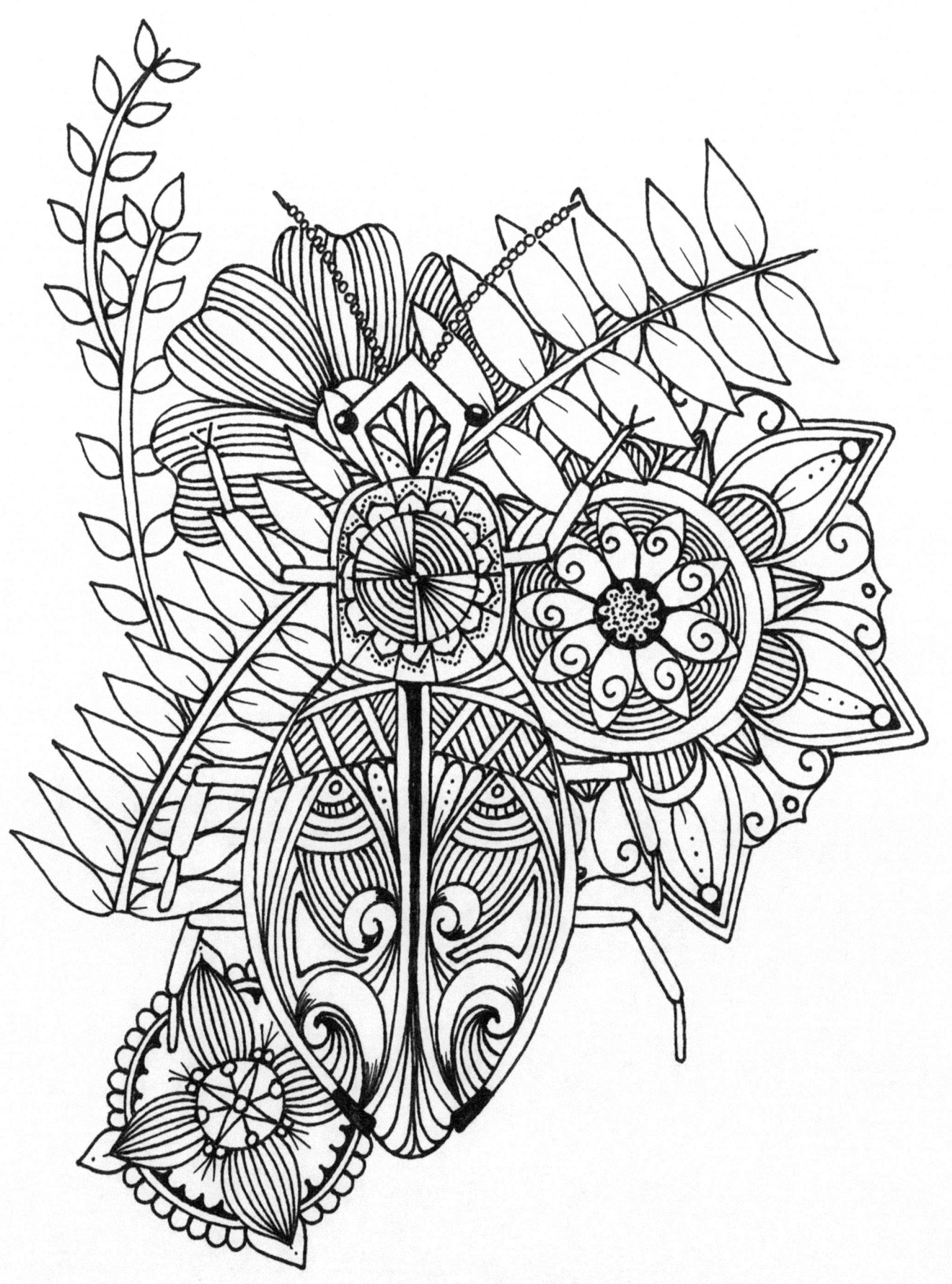

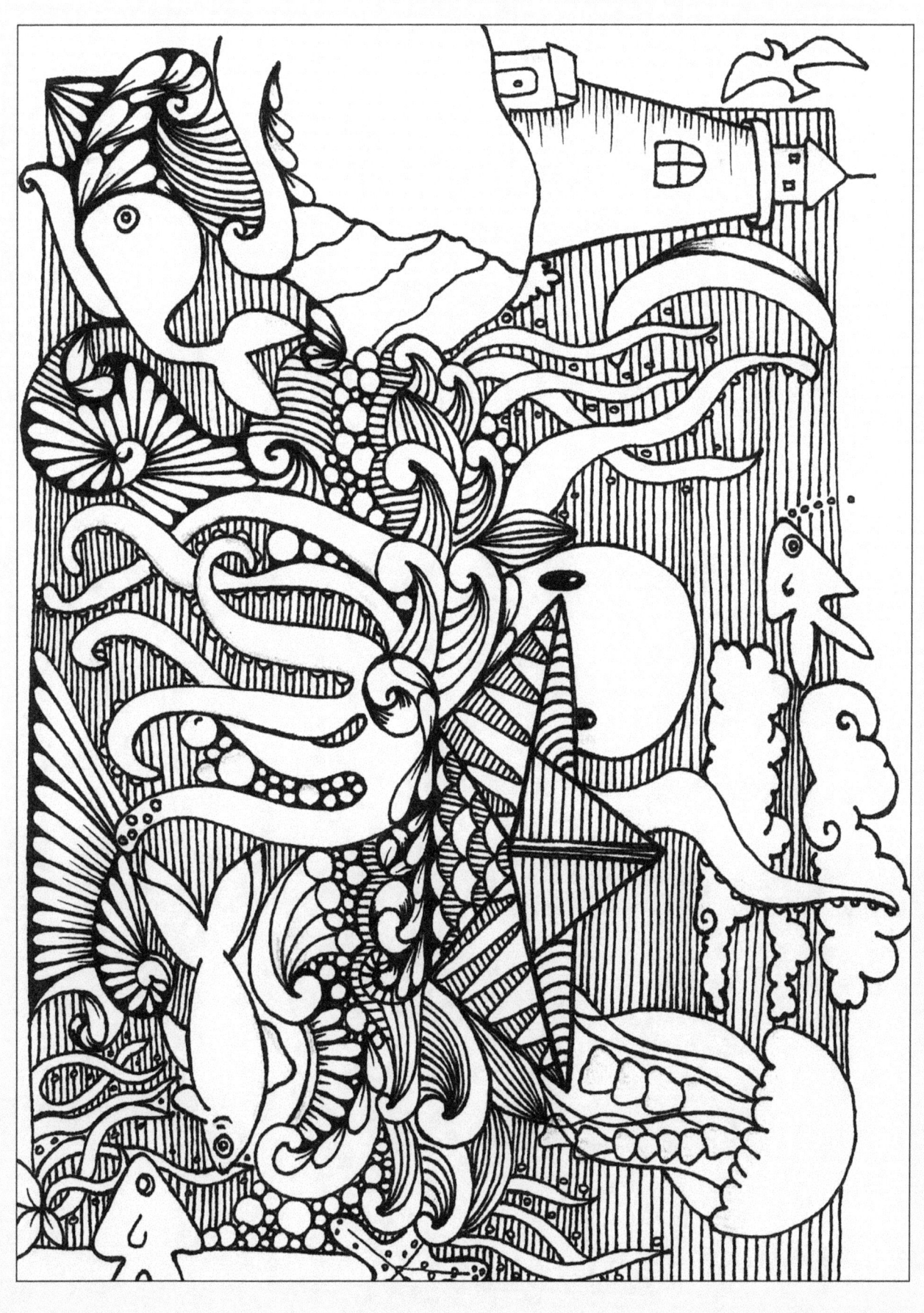

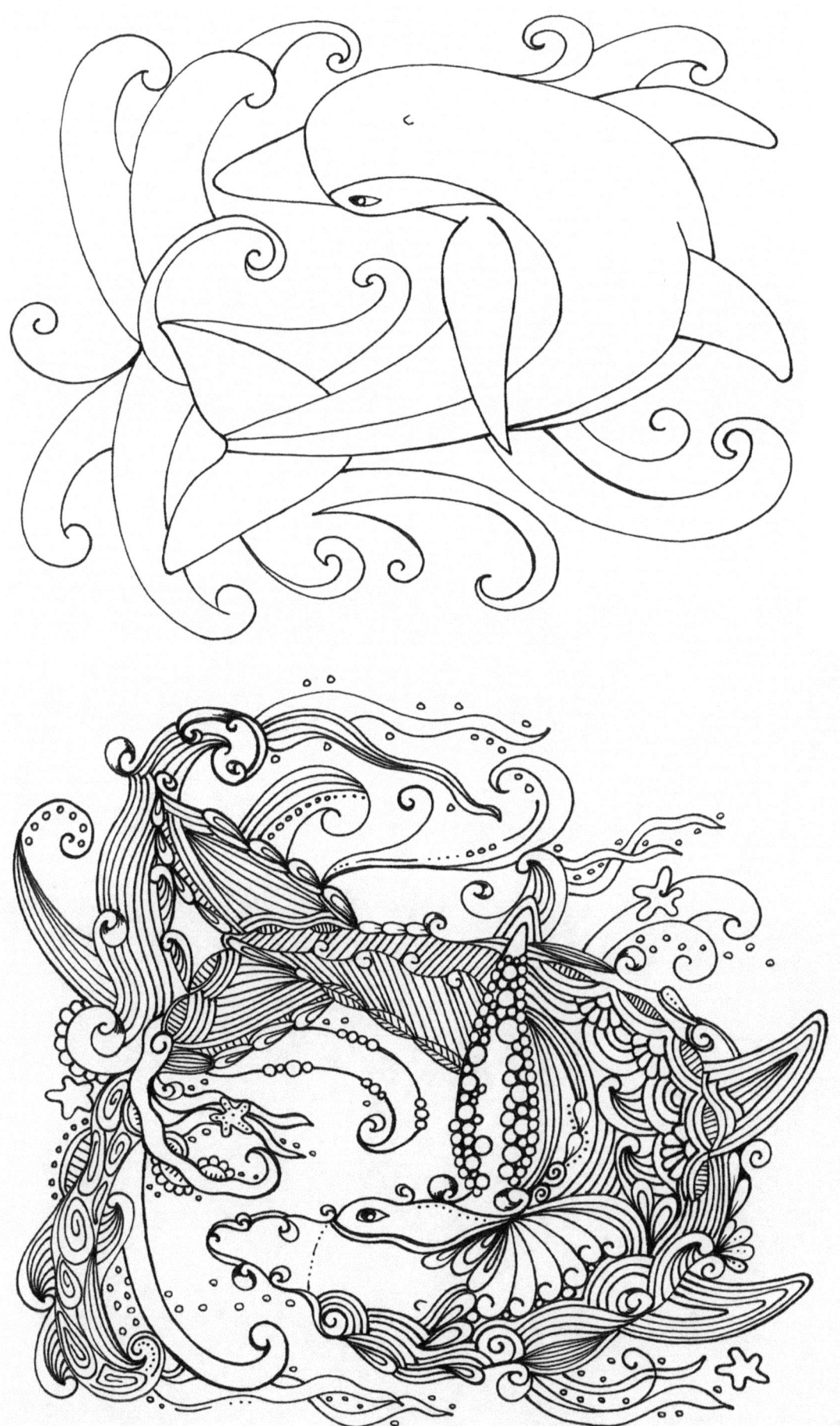

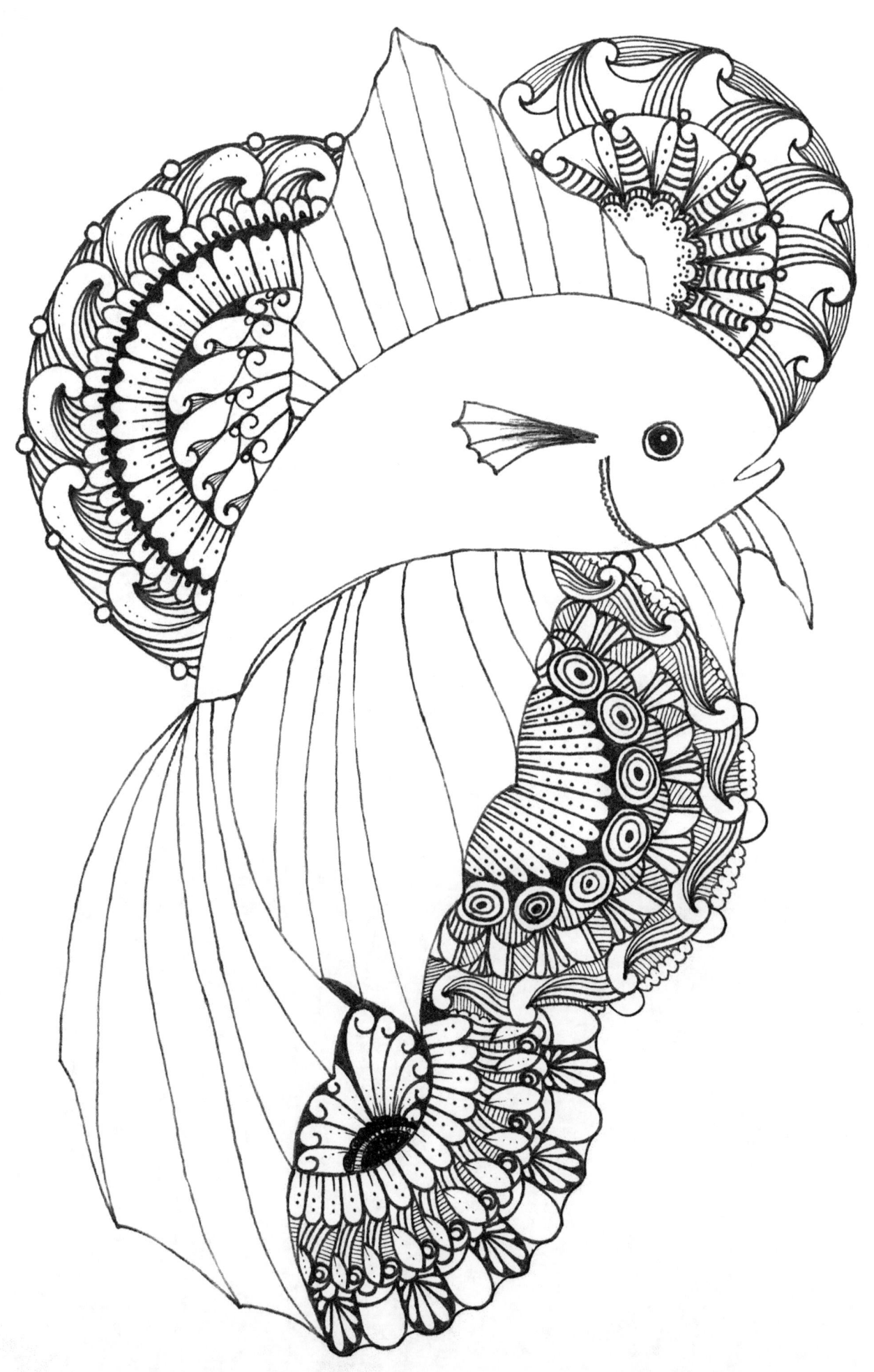

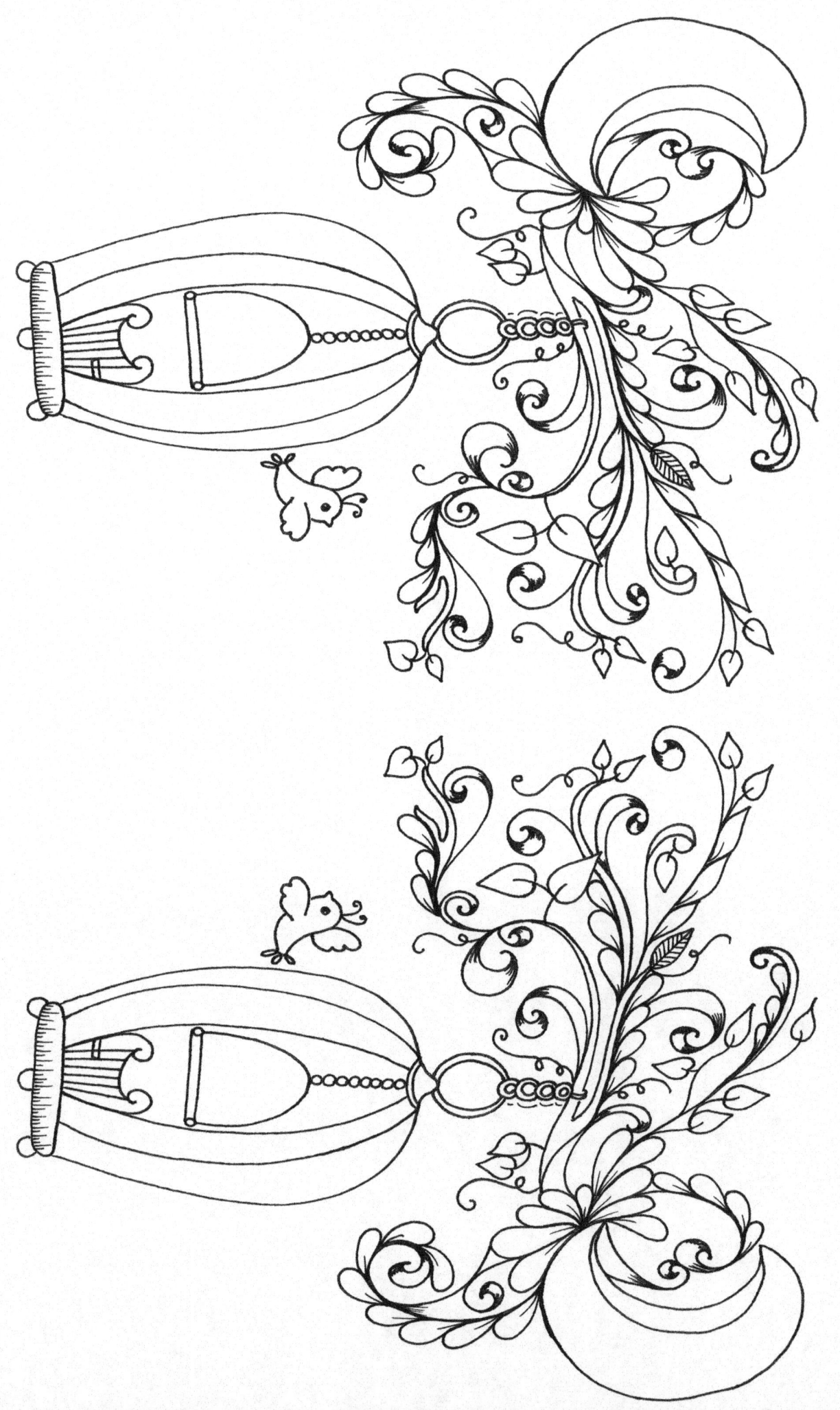

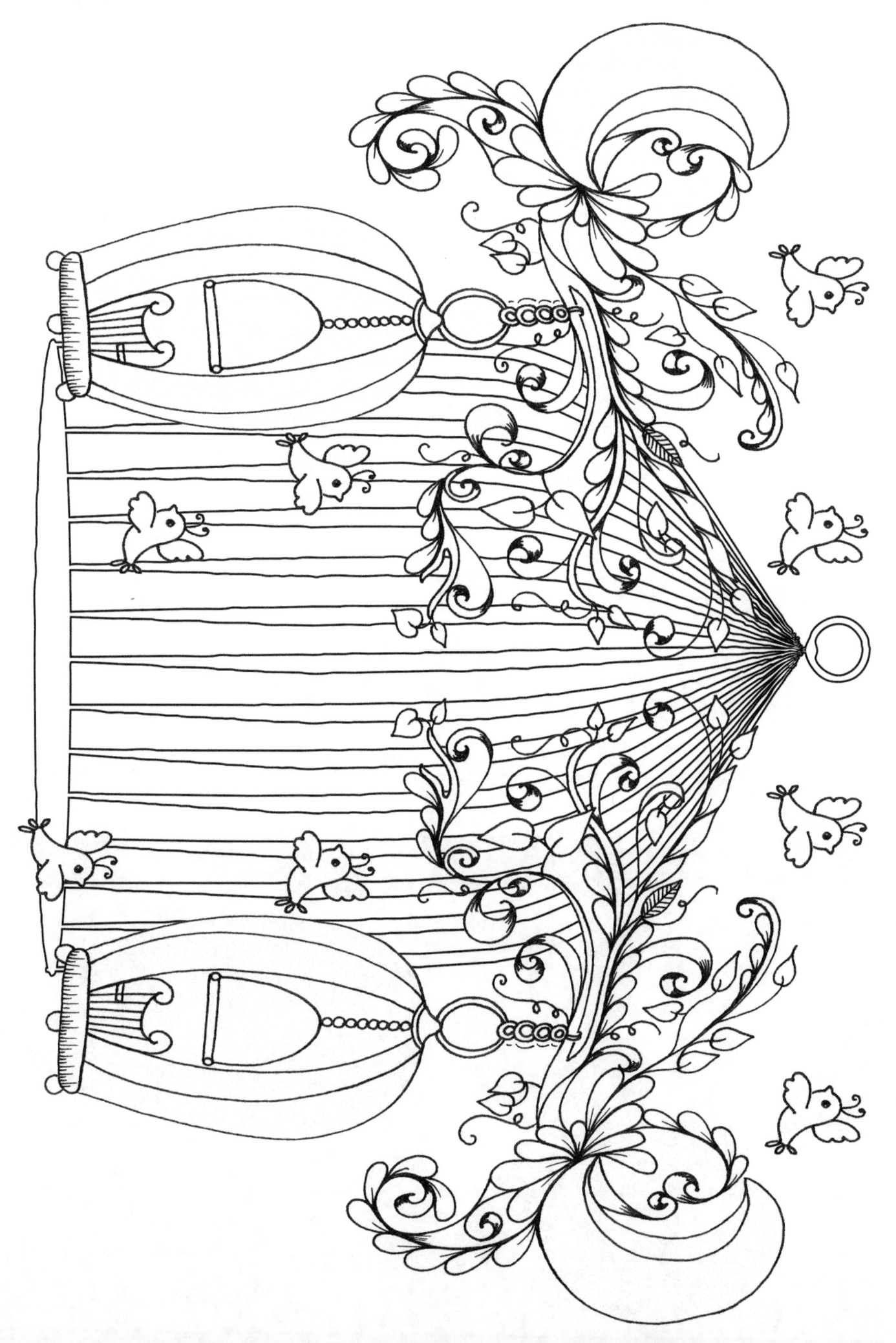

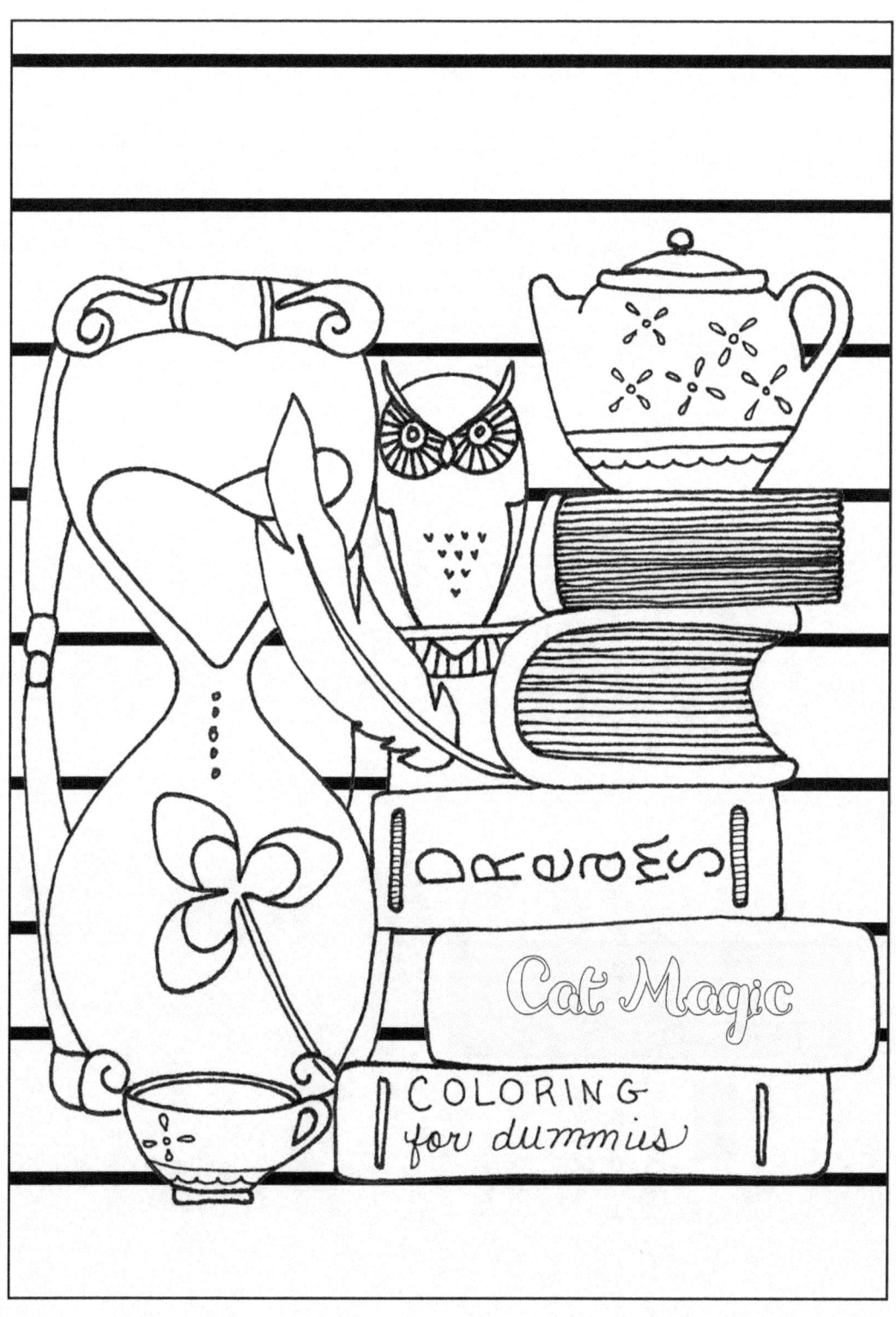

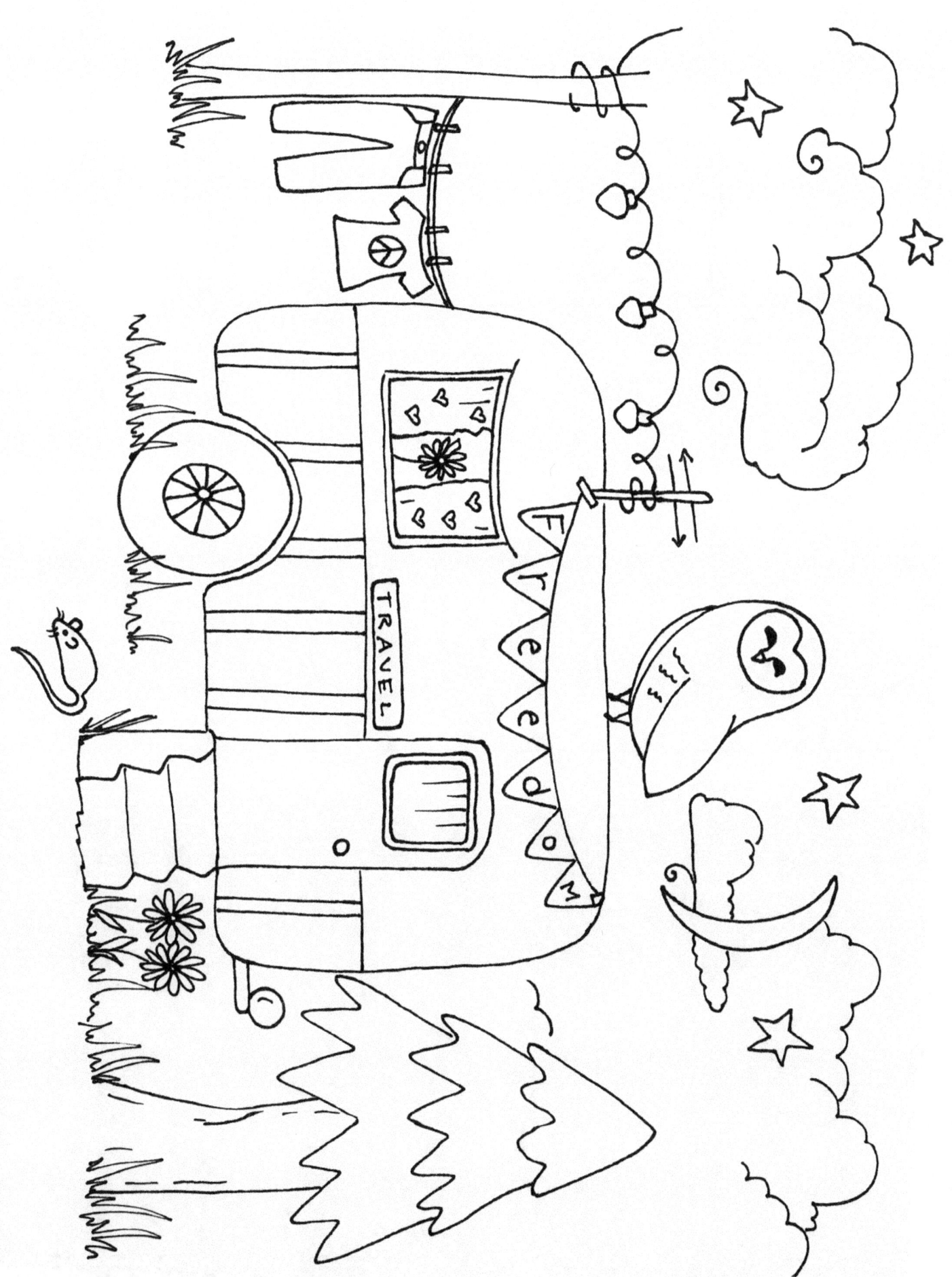

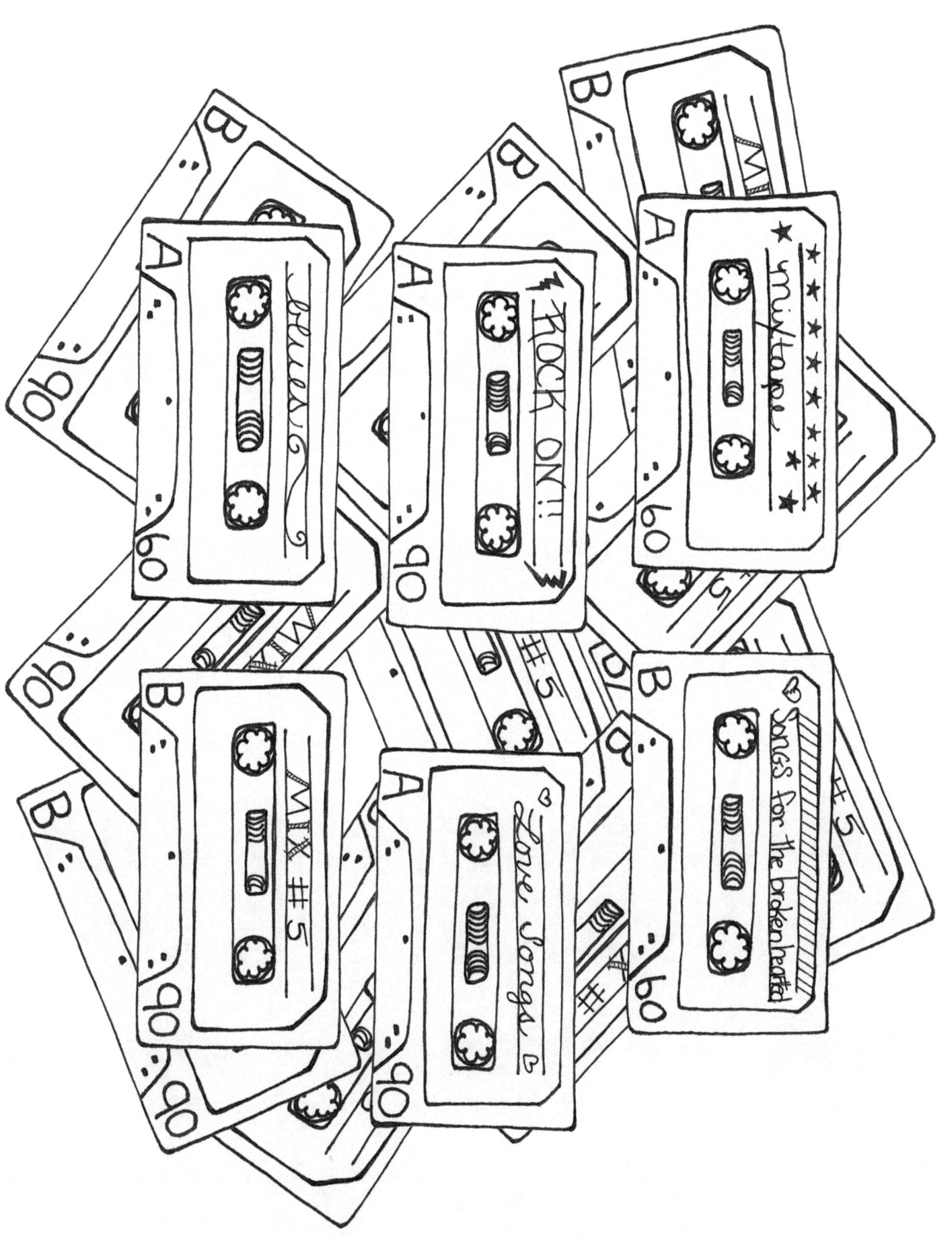

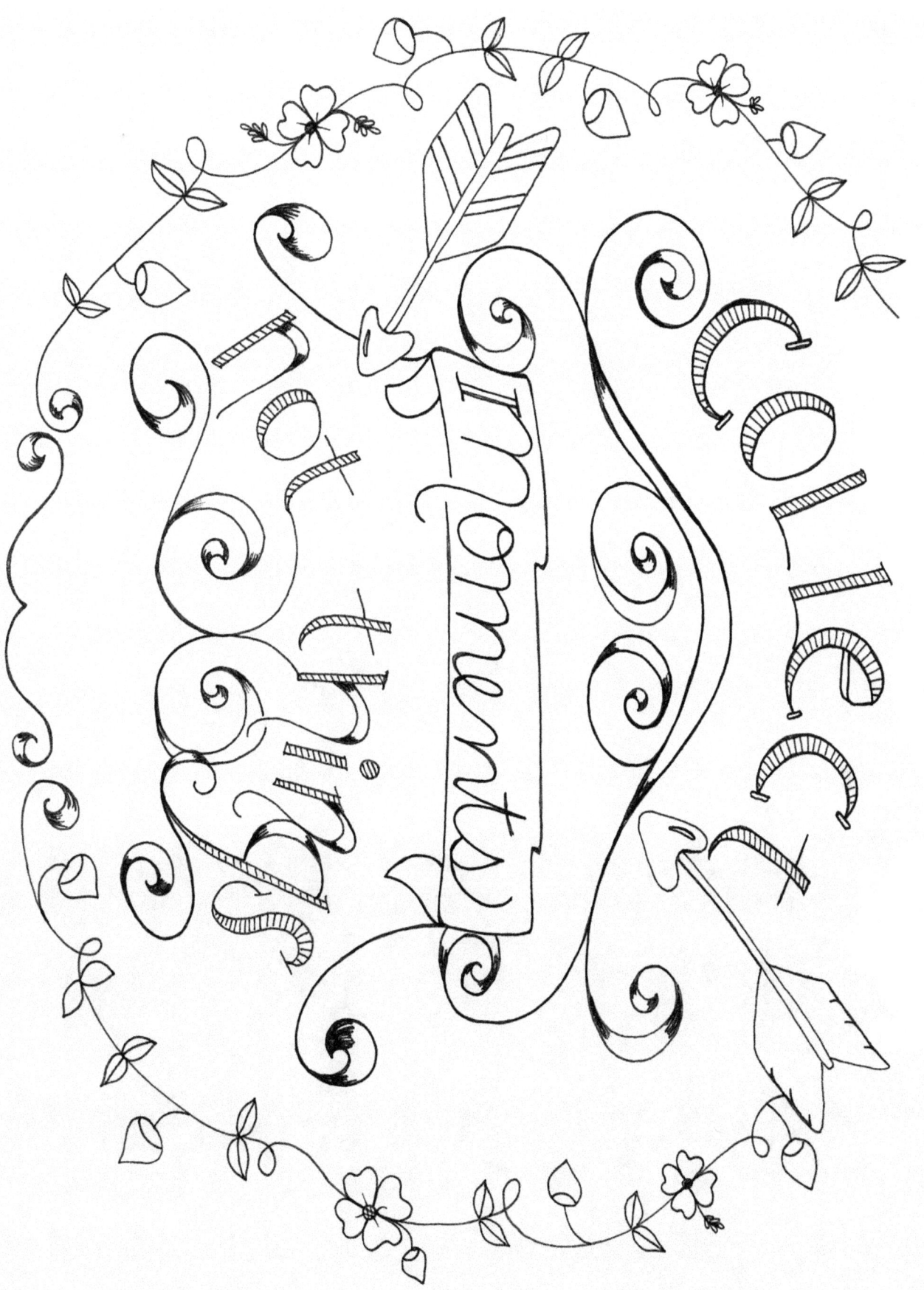

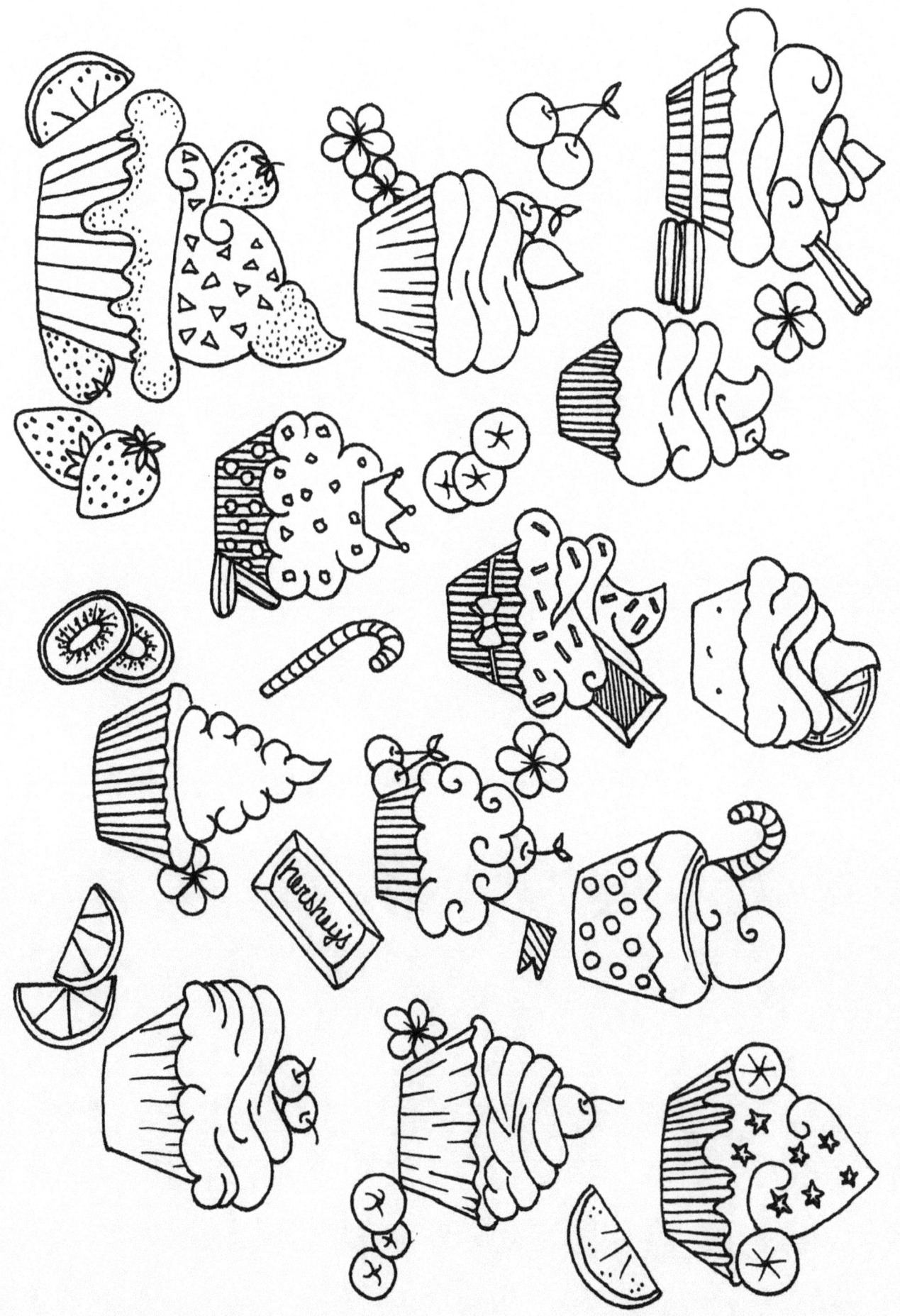

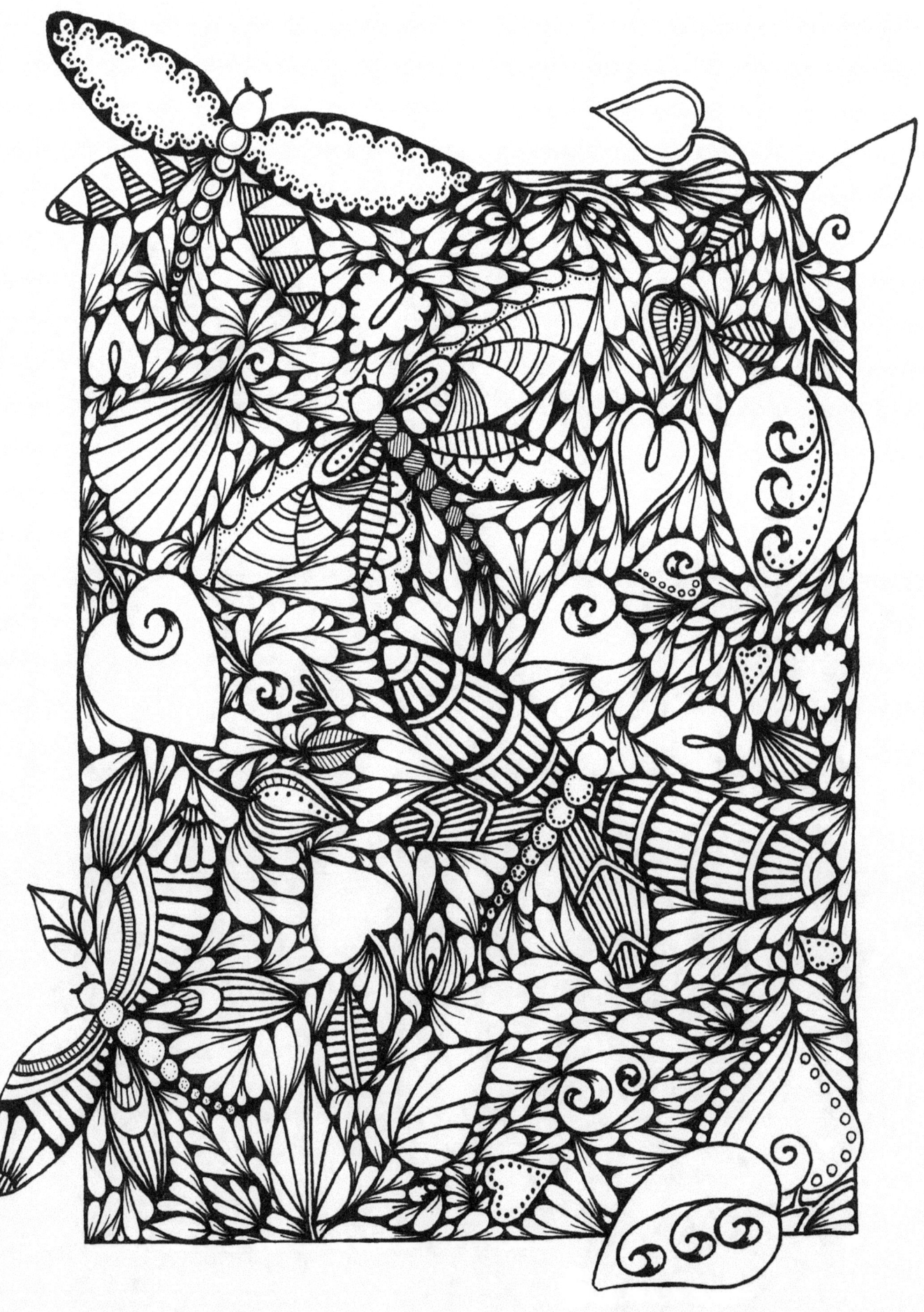

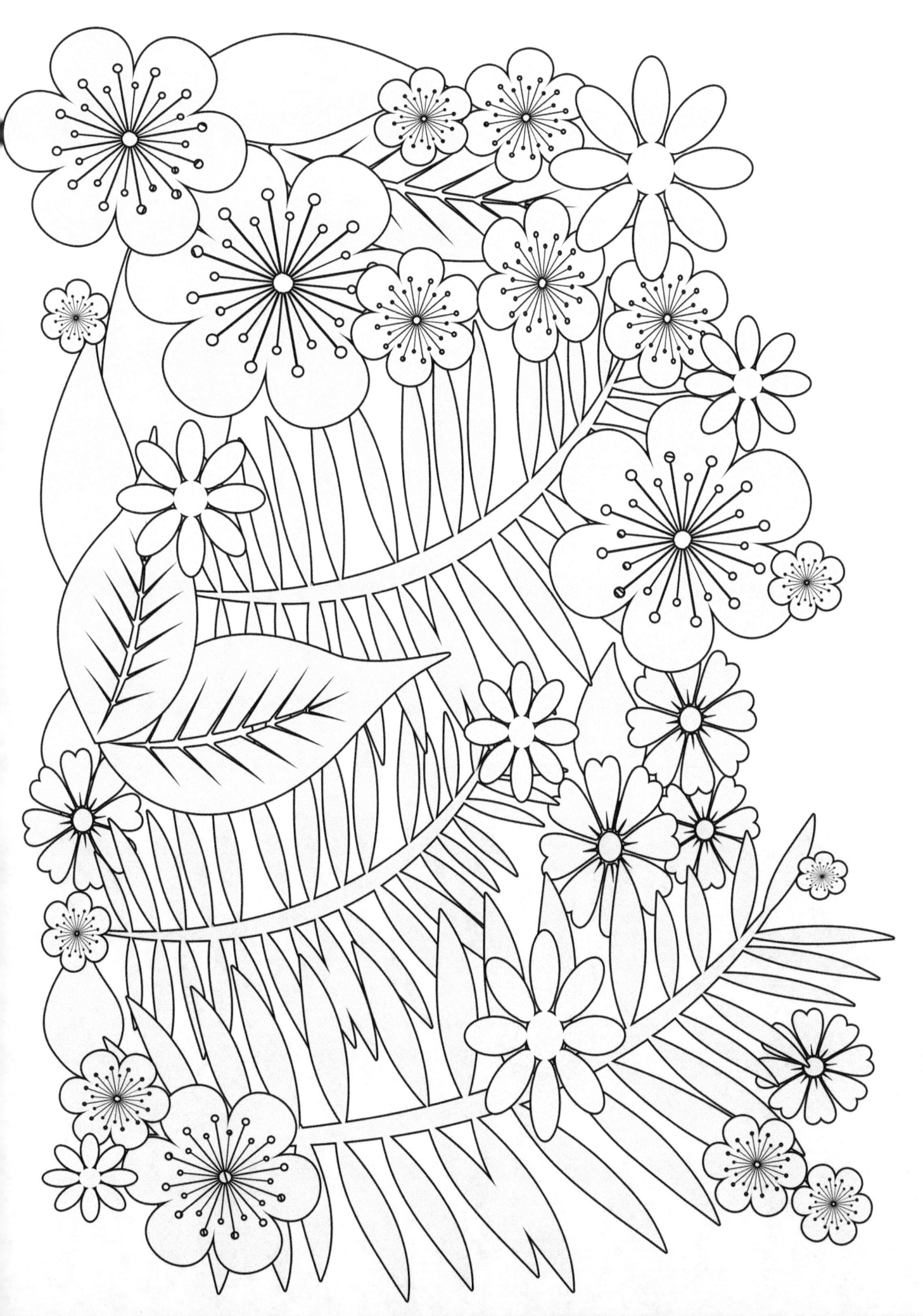

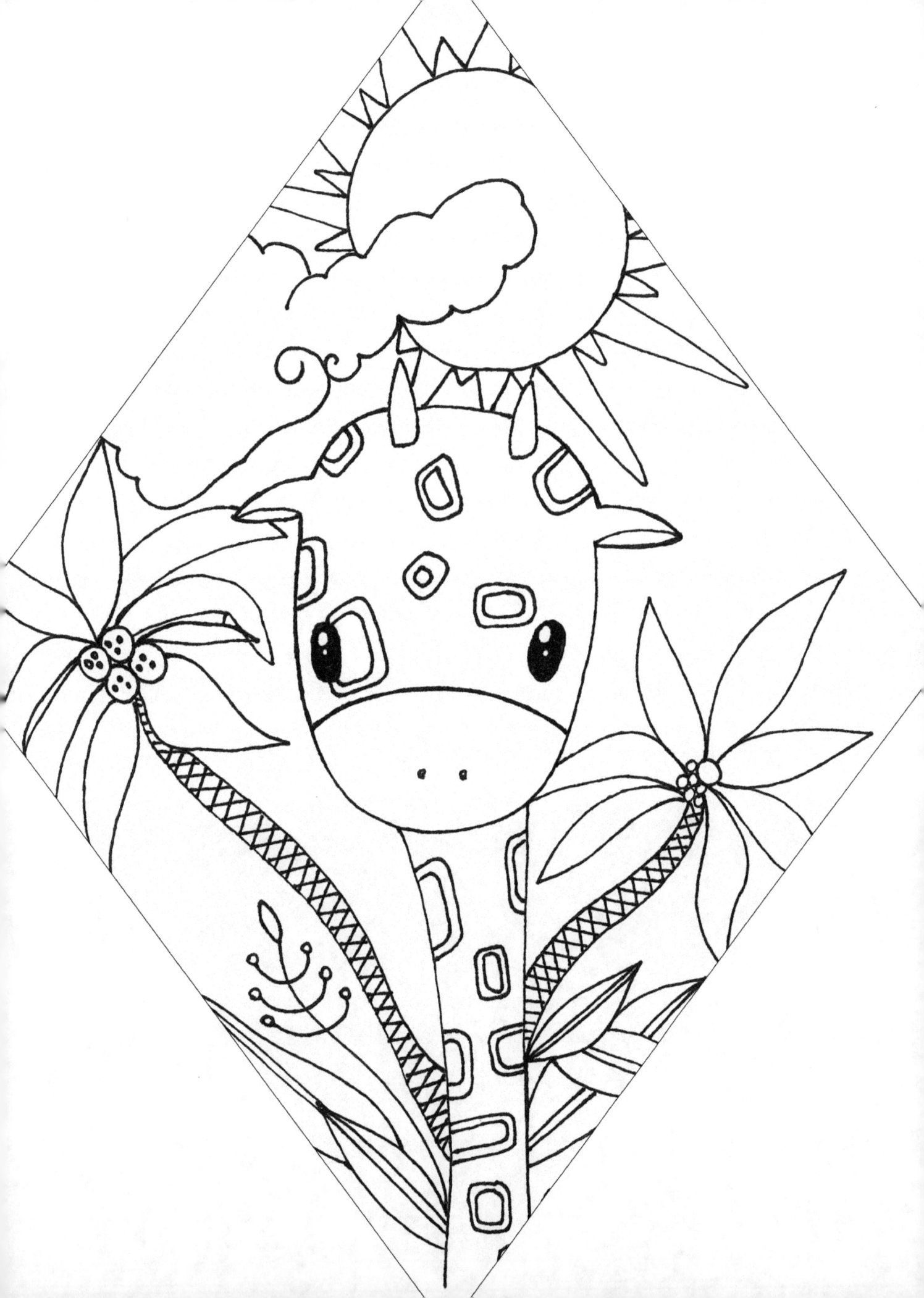

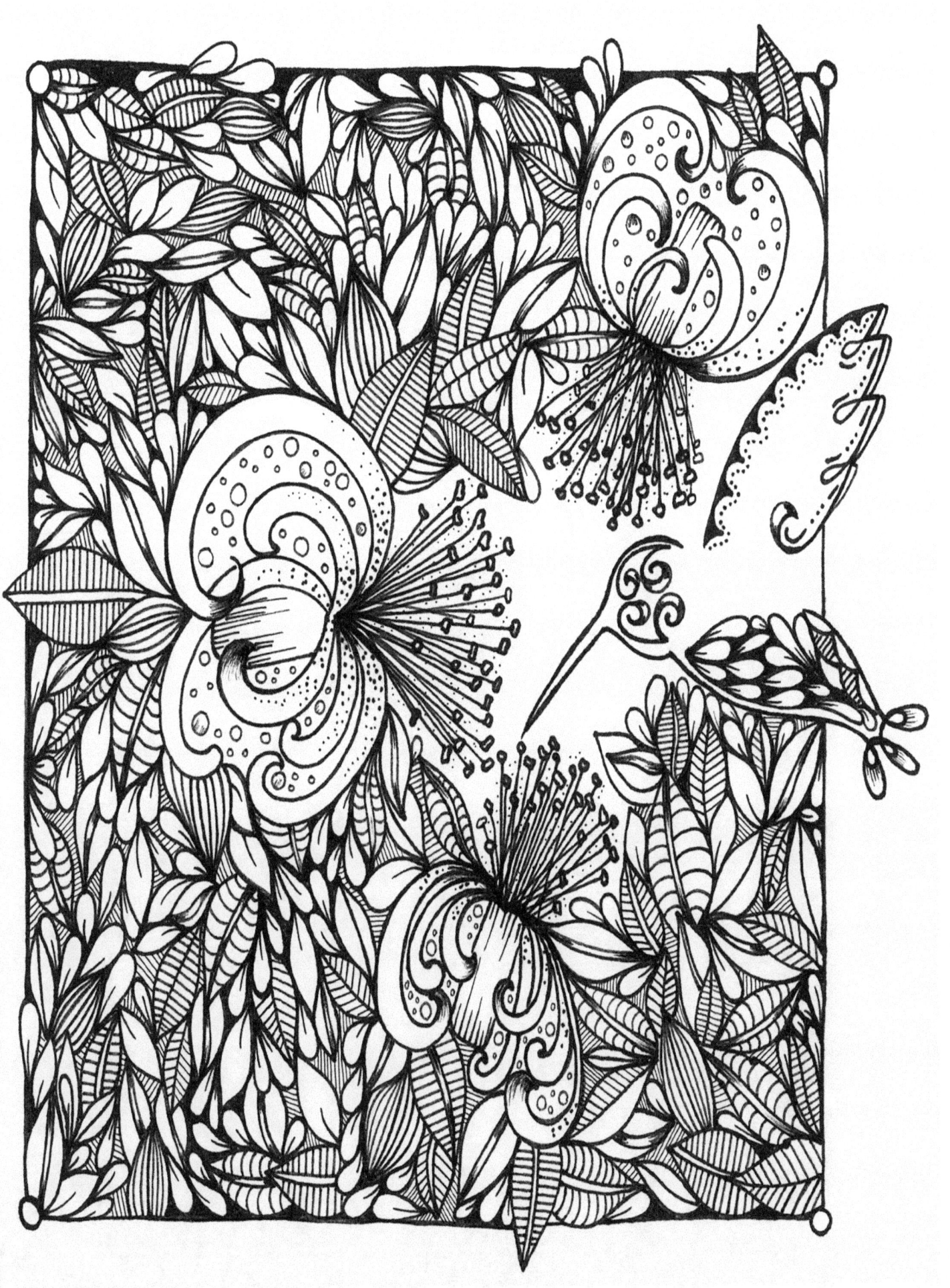

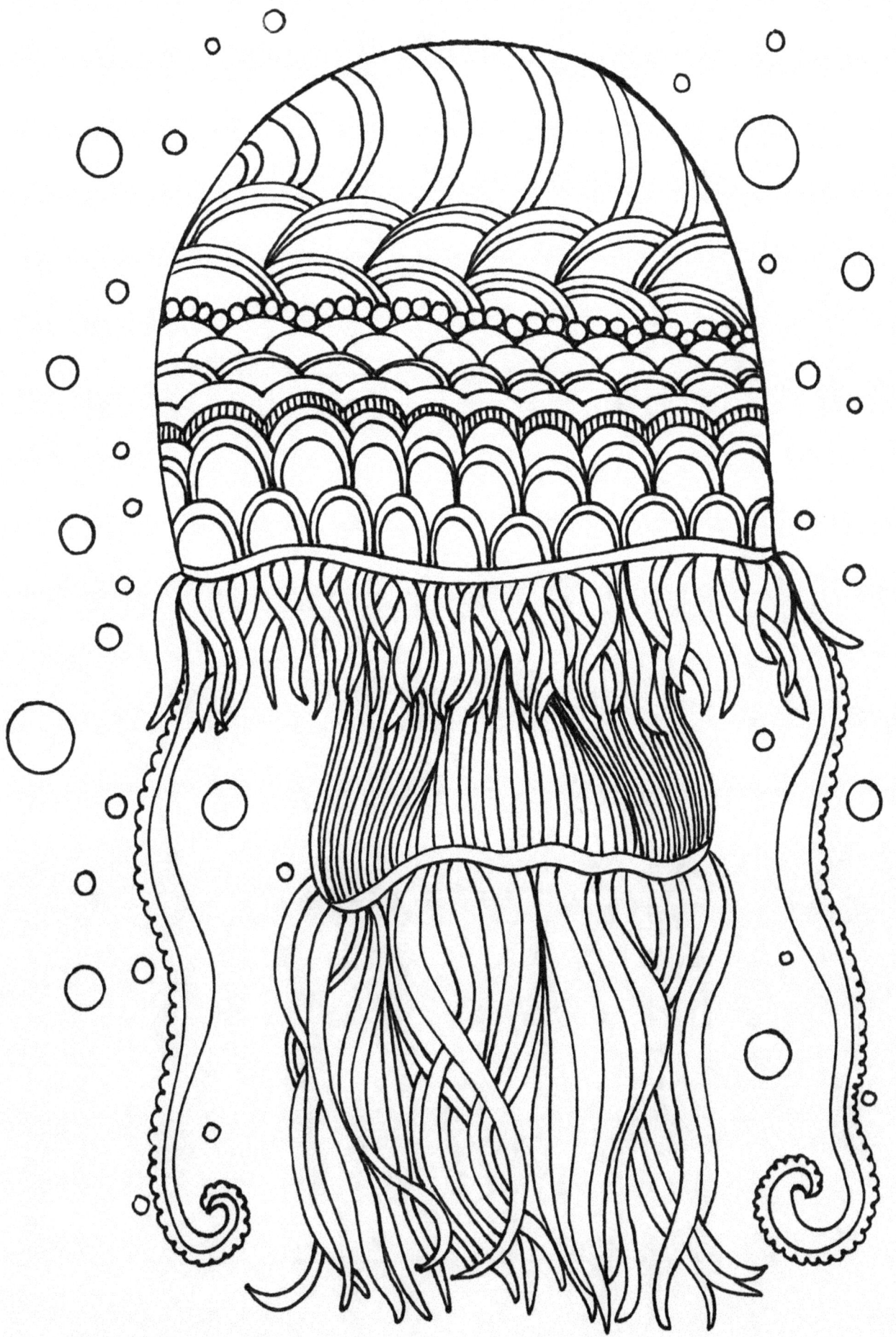

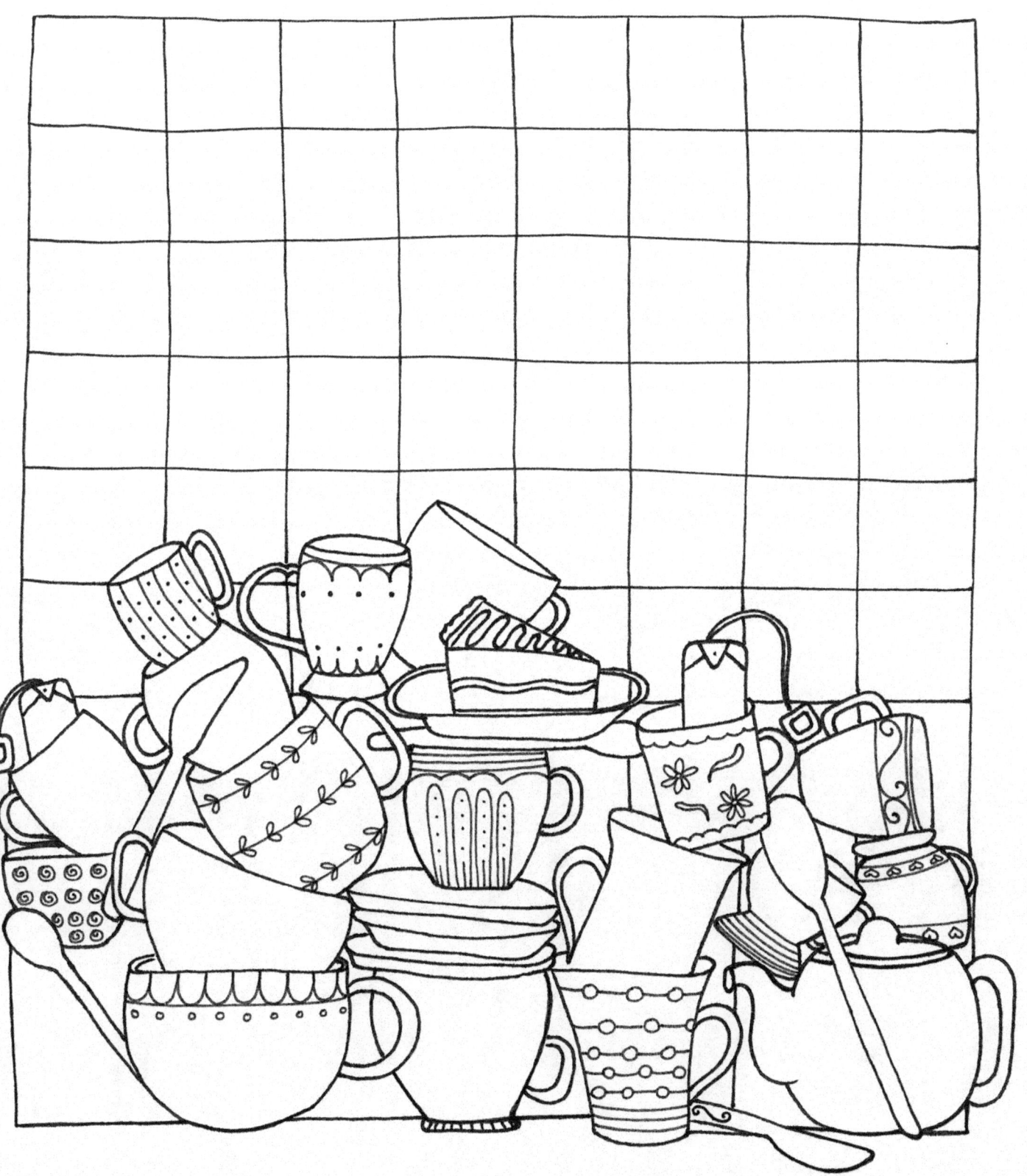

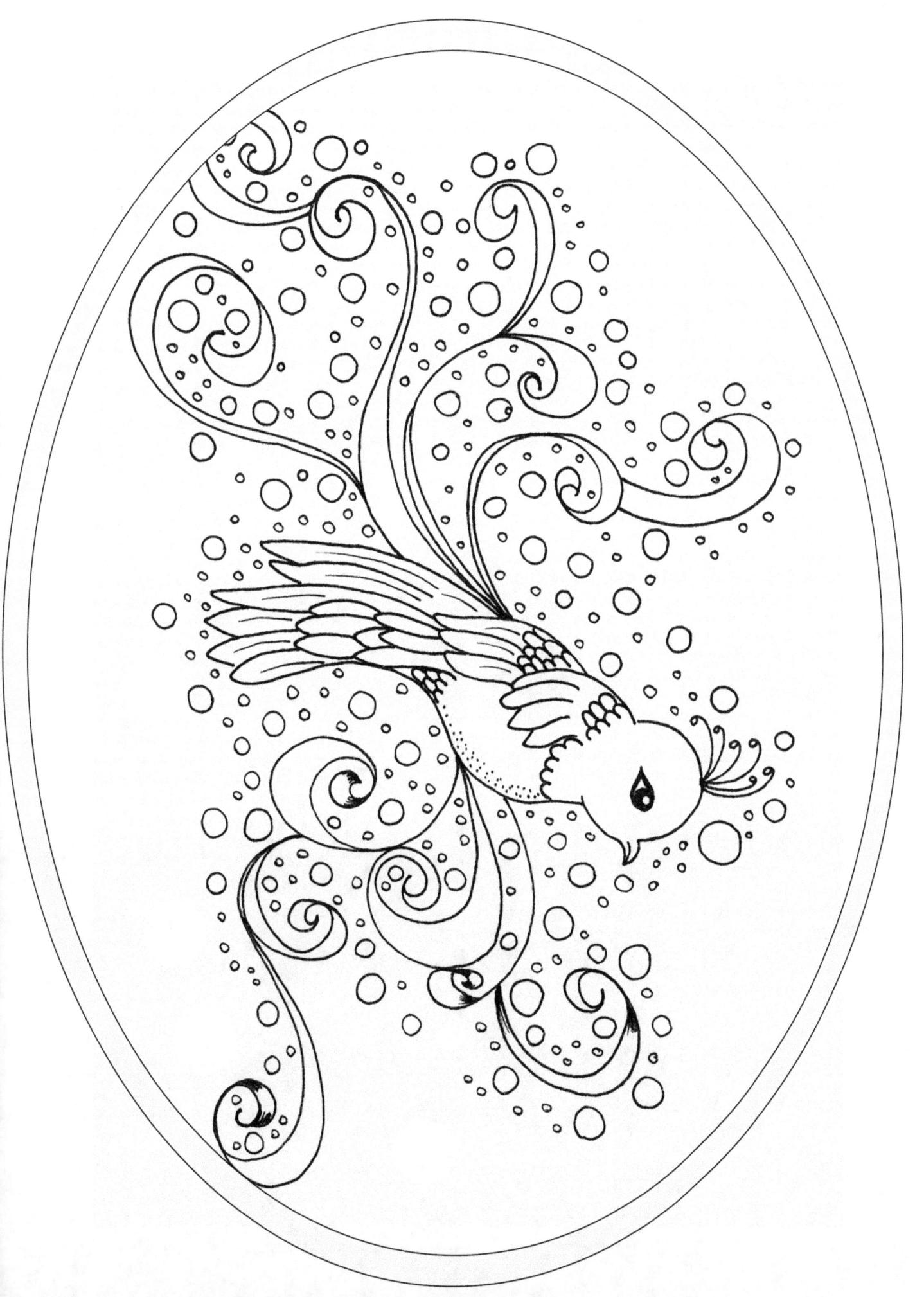

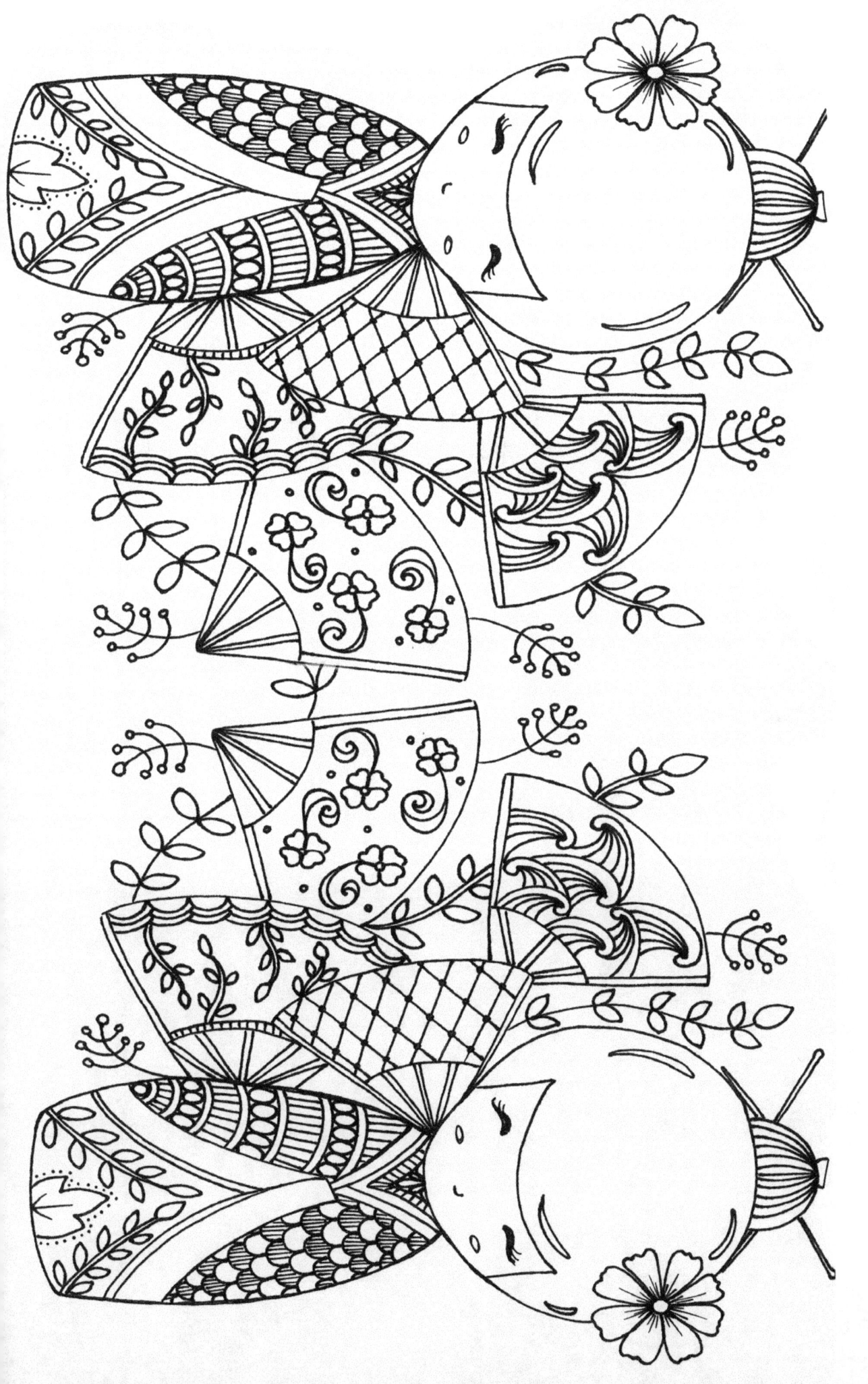

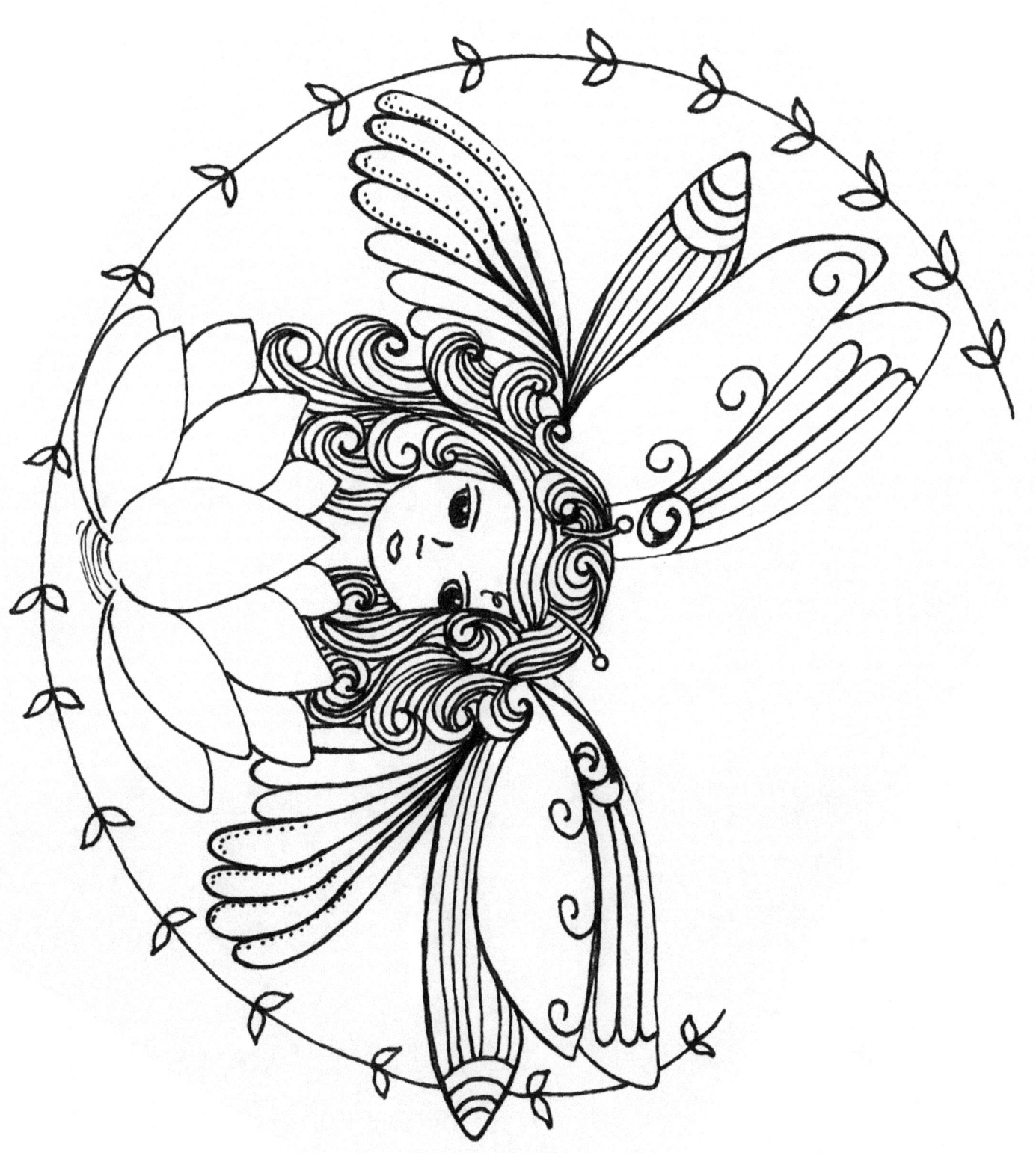

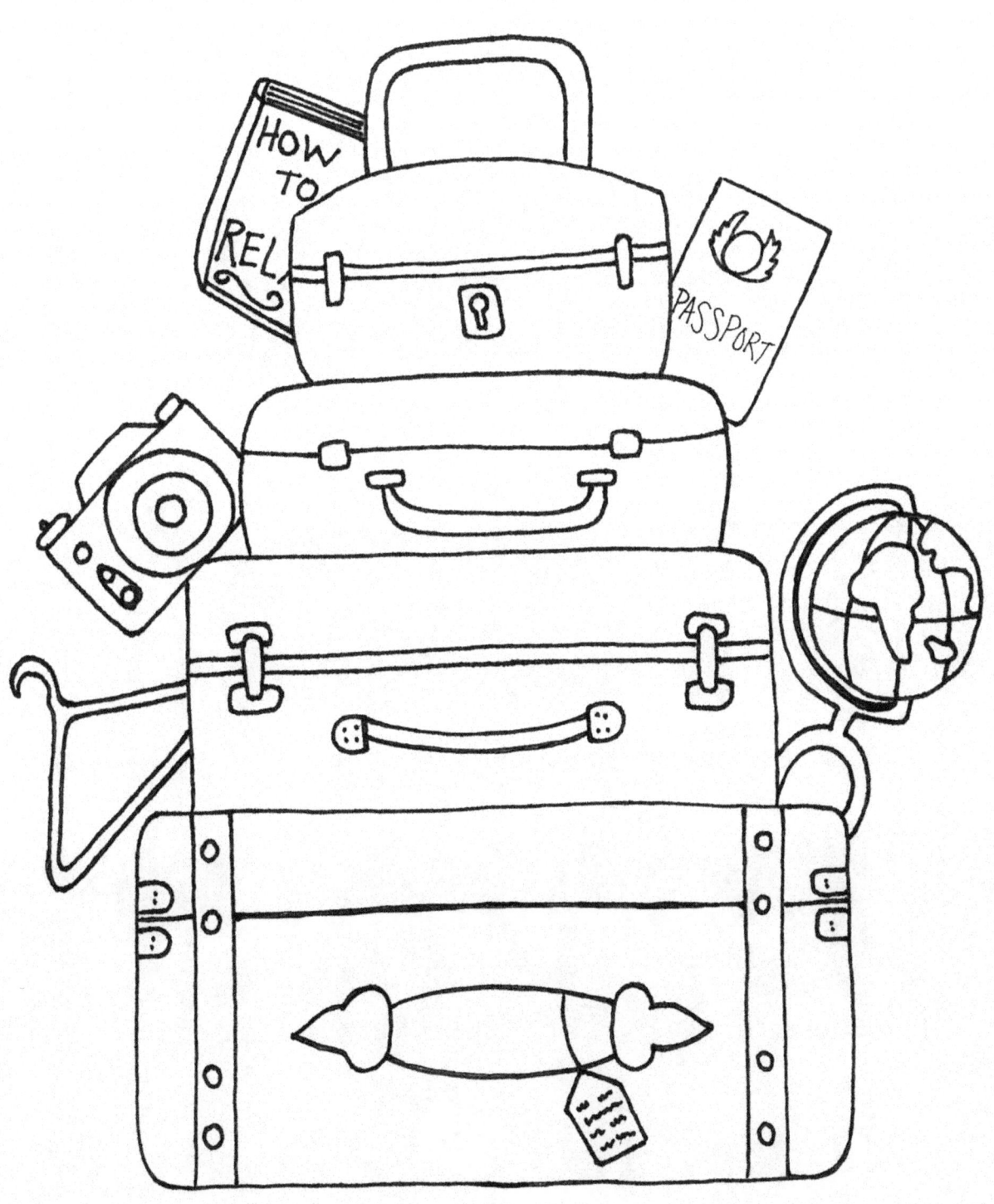

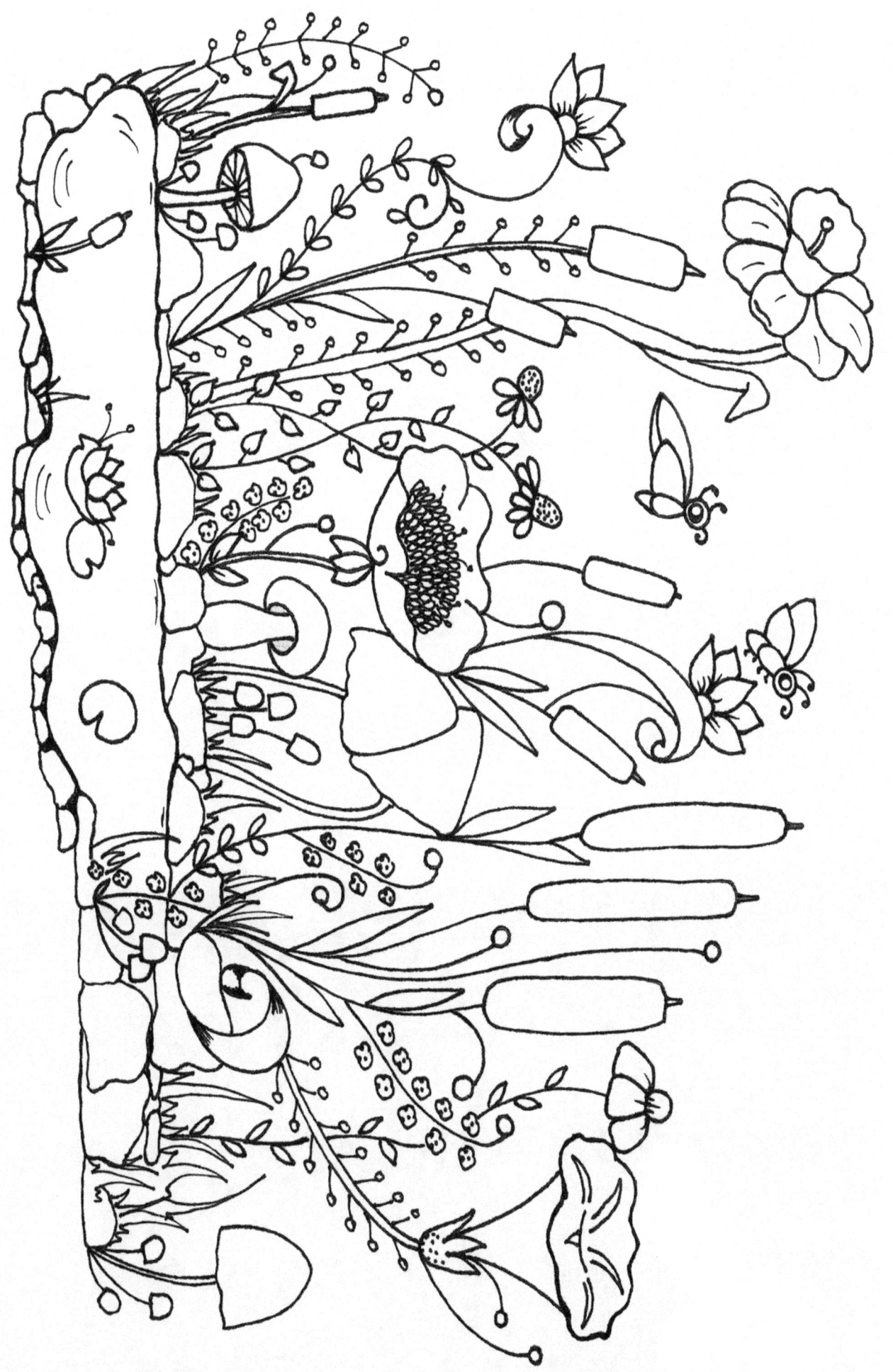

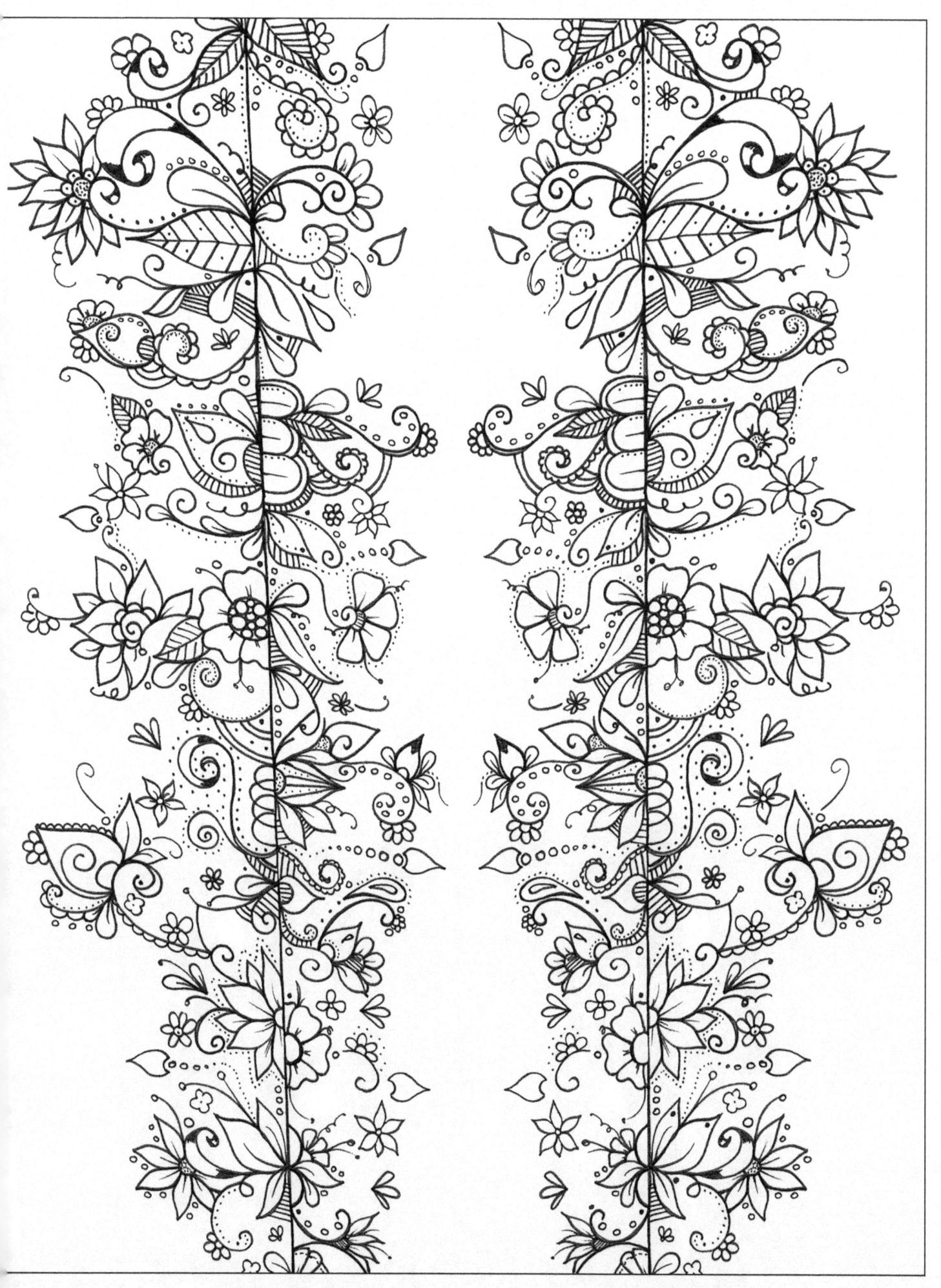

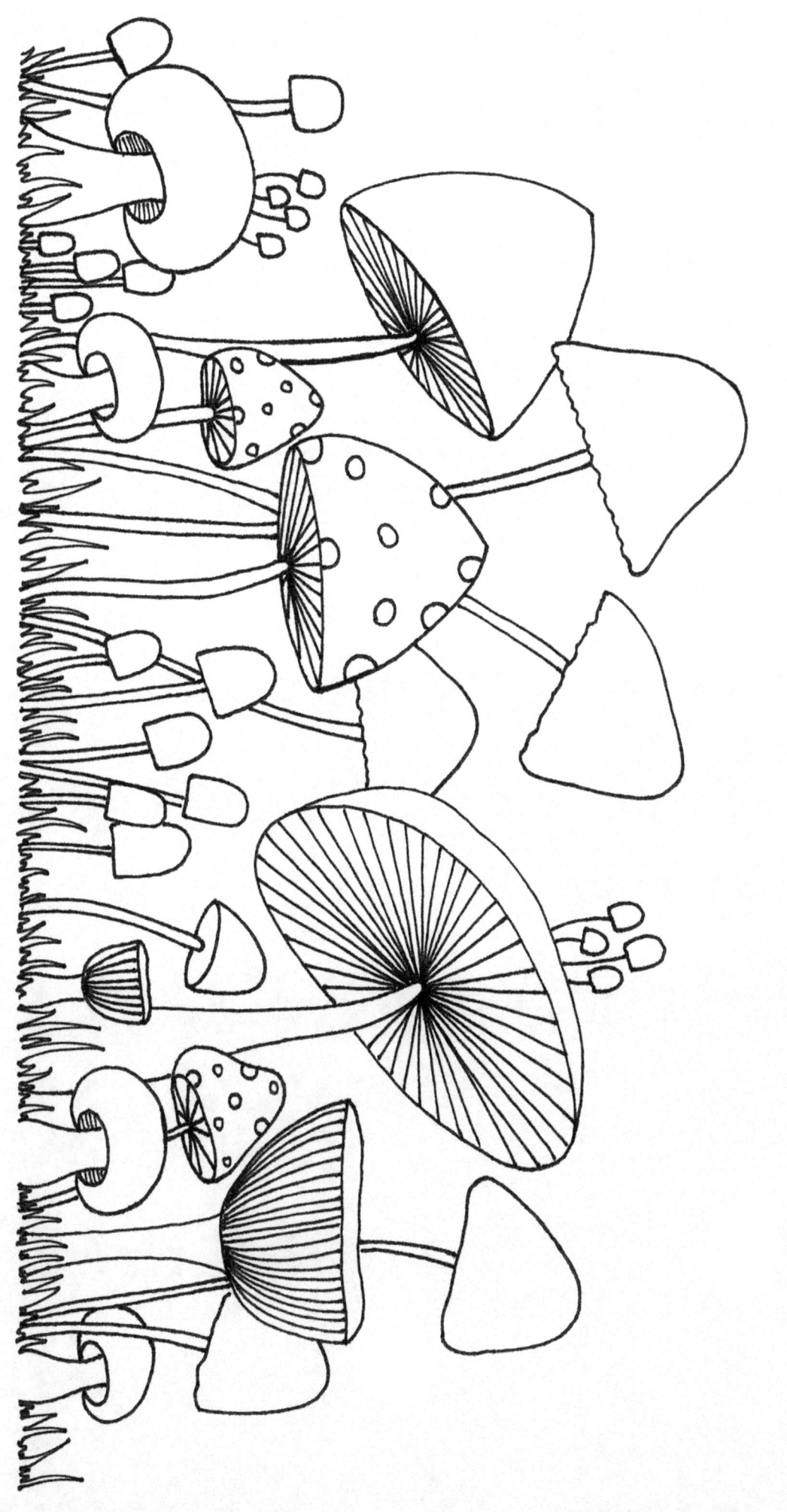

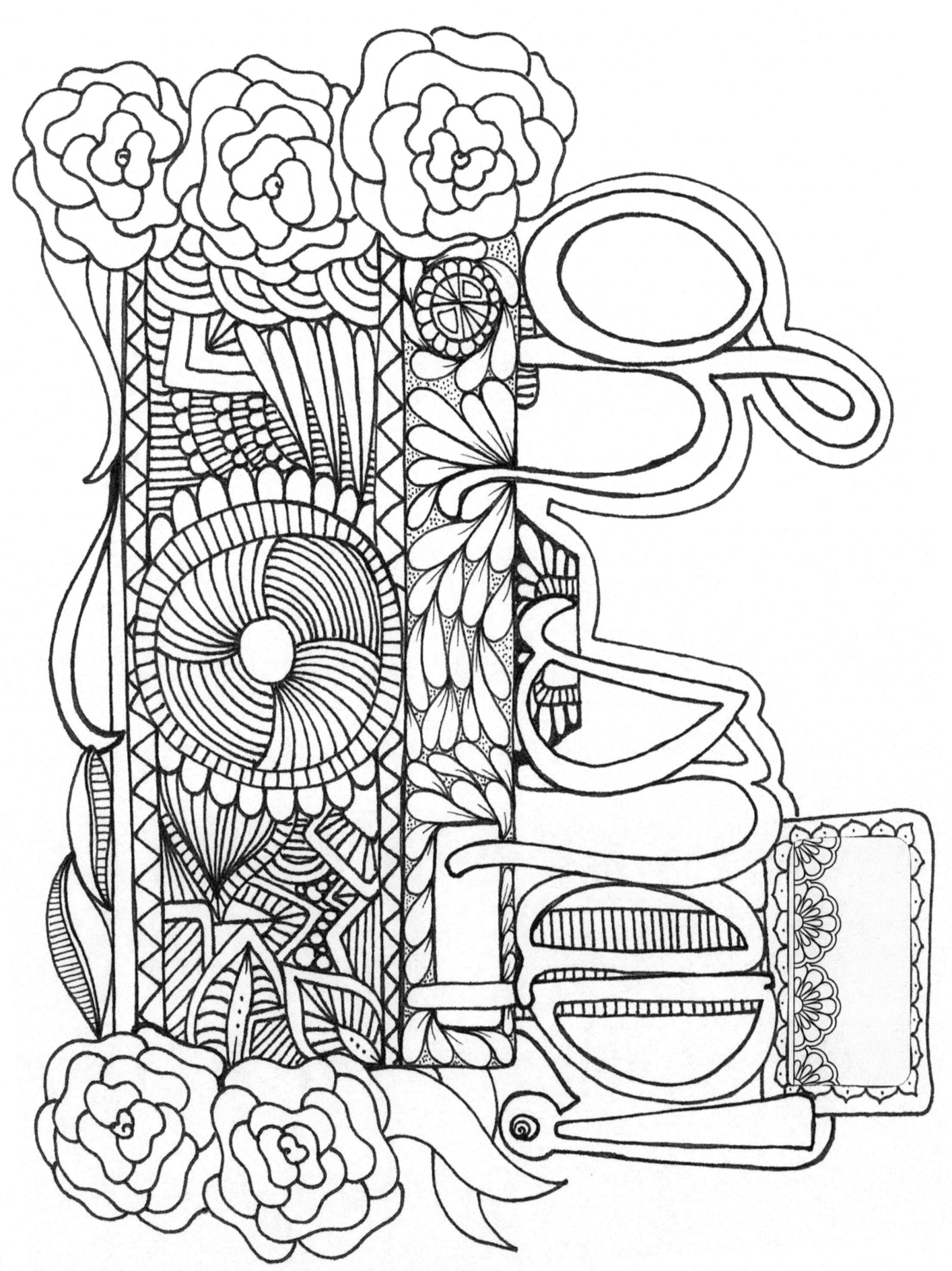

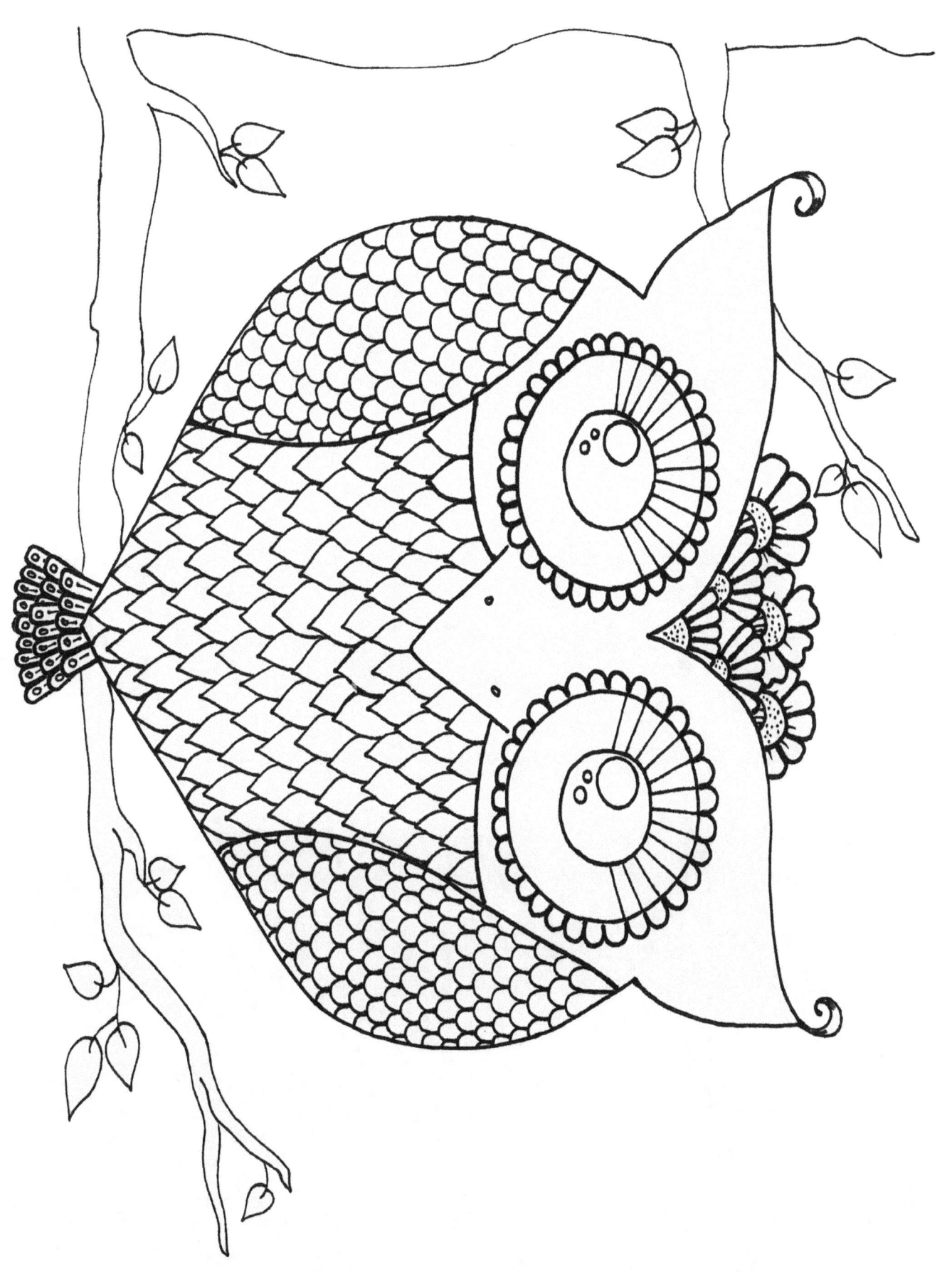

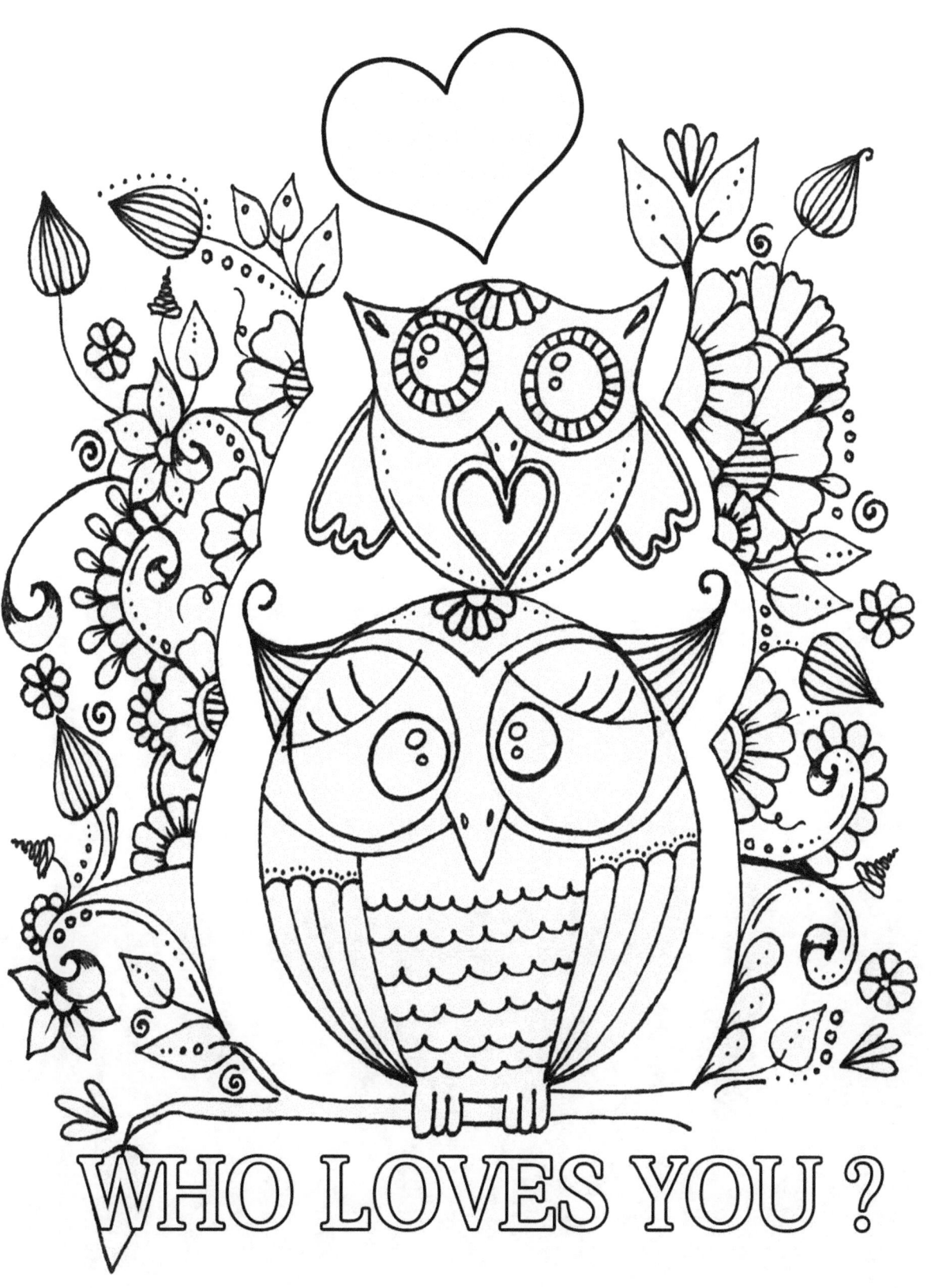

WHO LOVES YOU ?

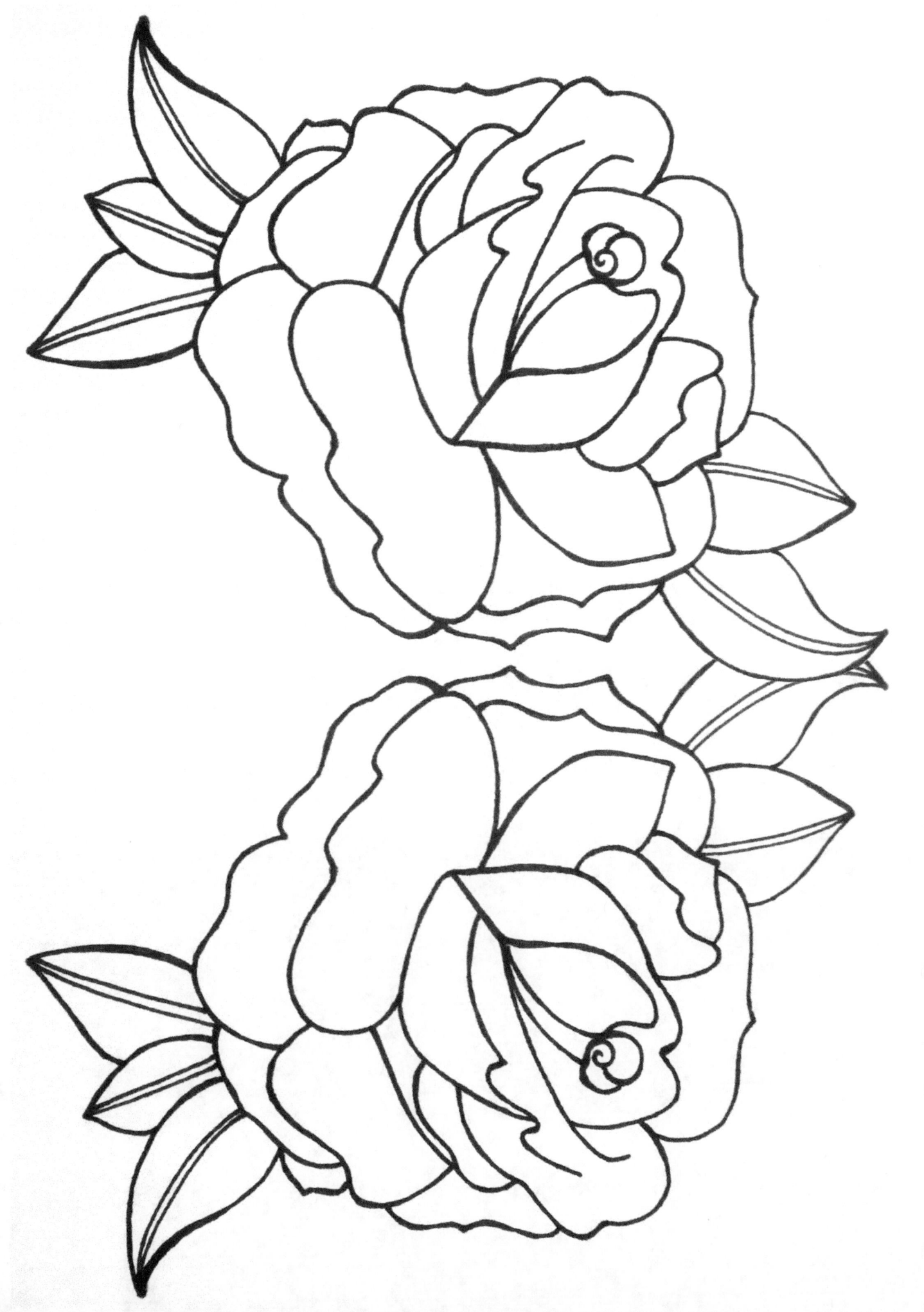

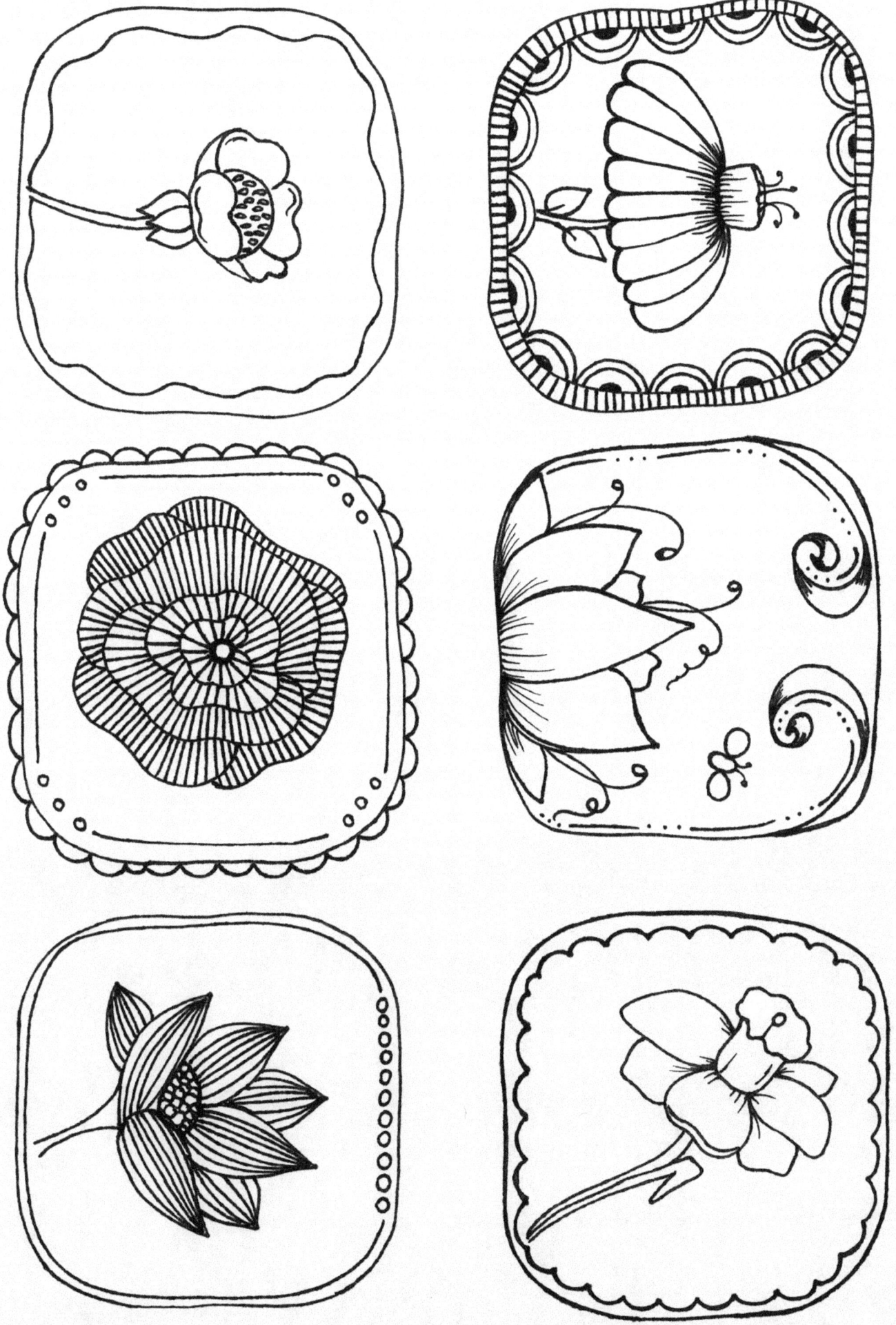

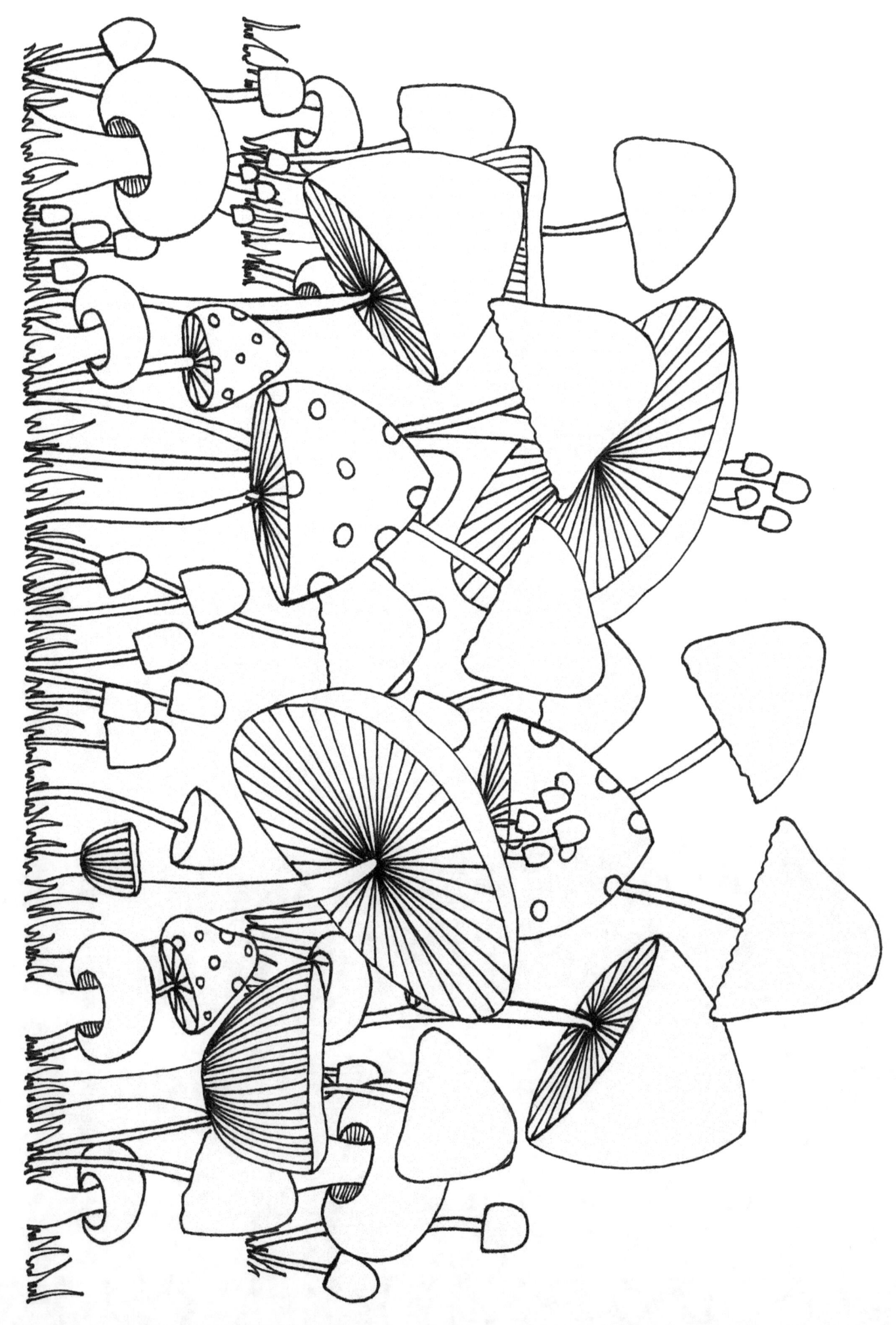

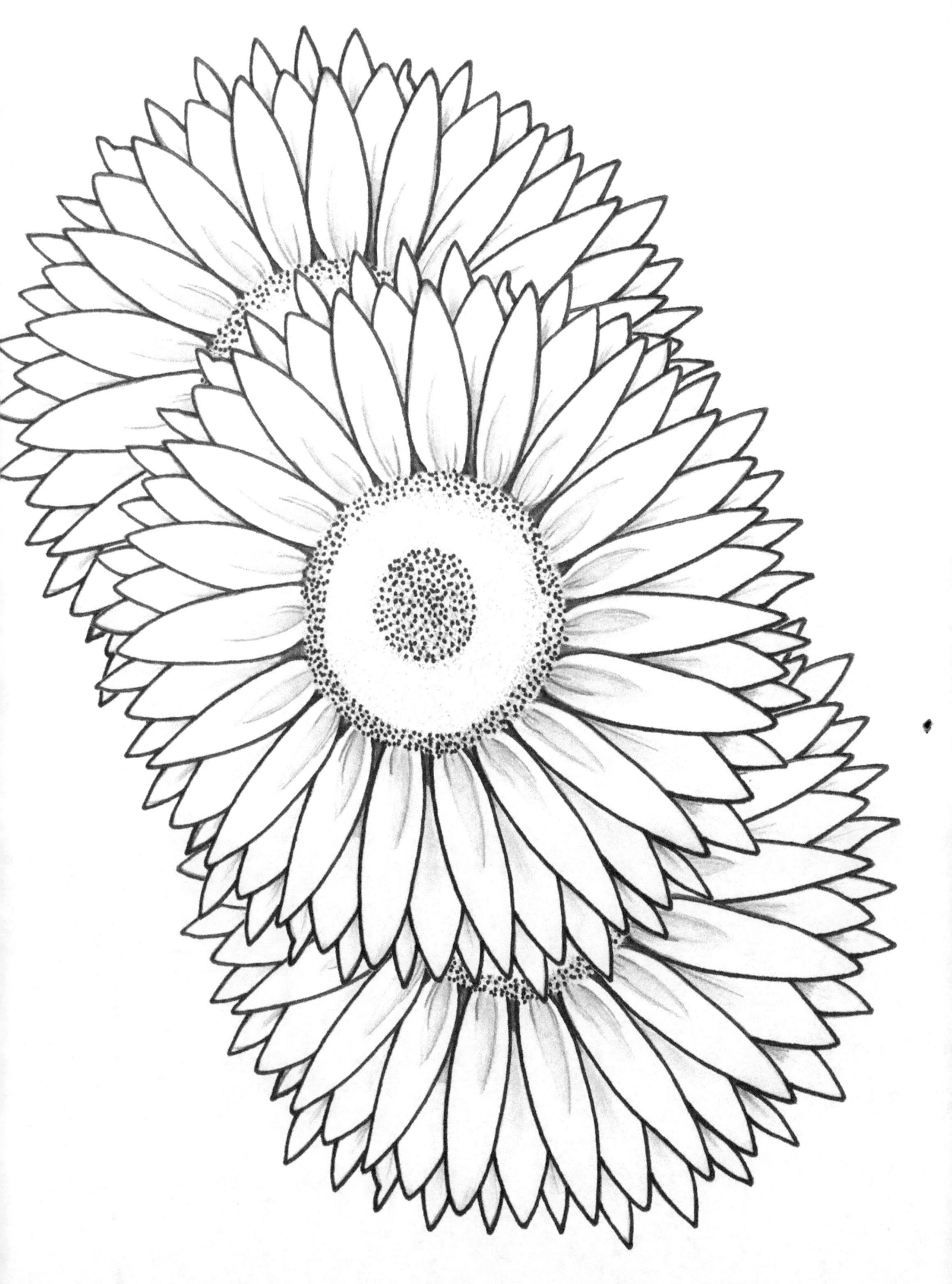

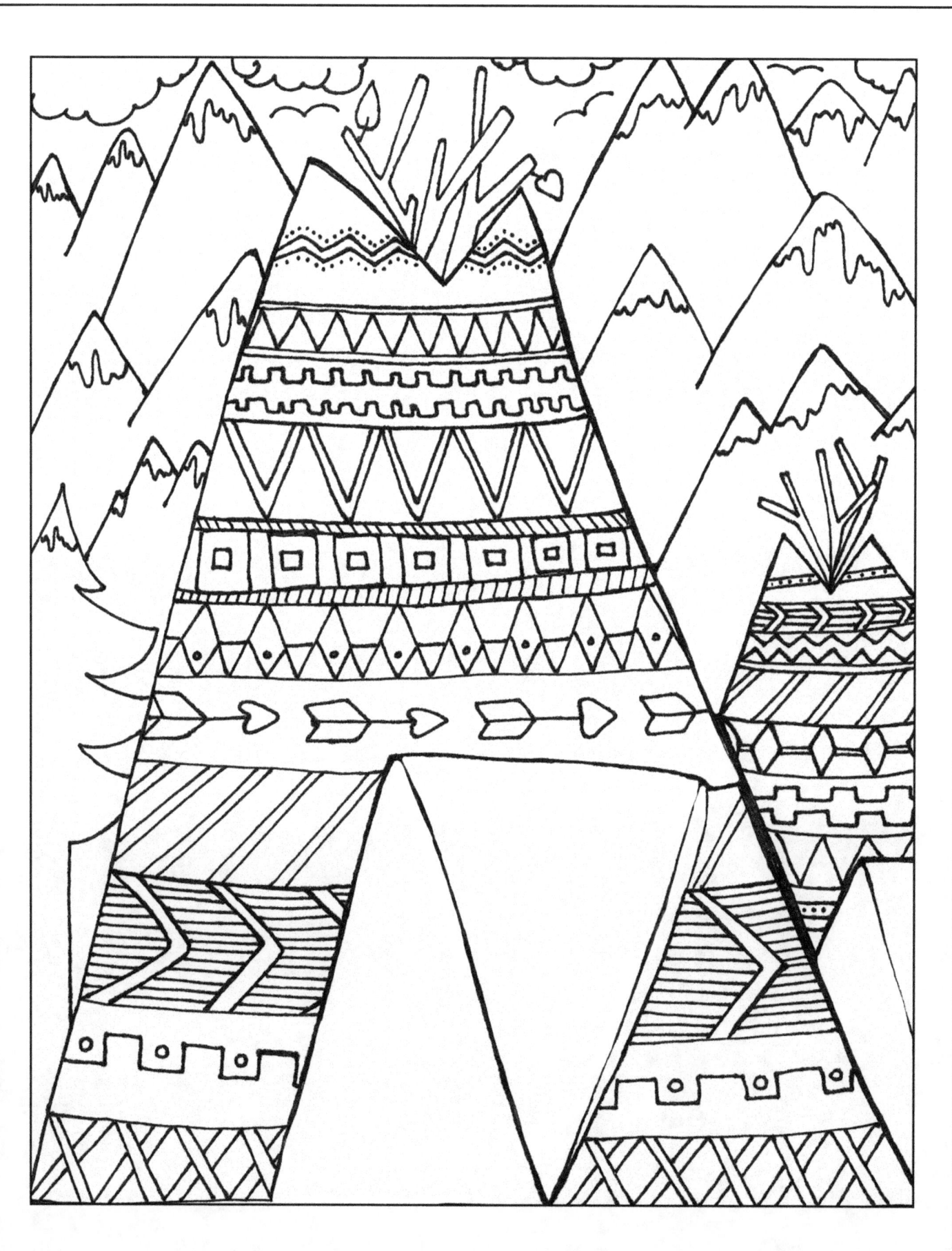

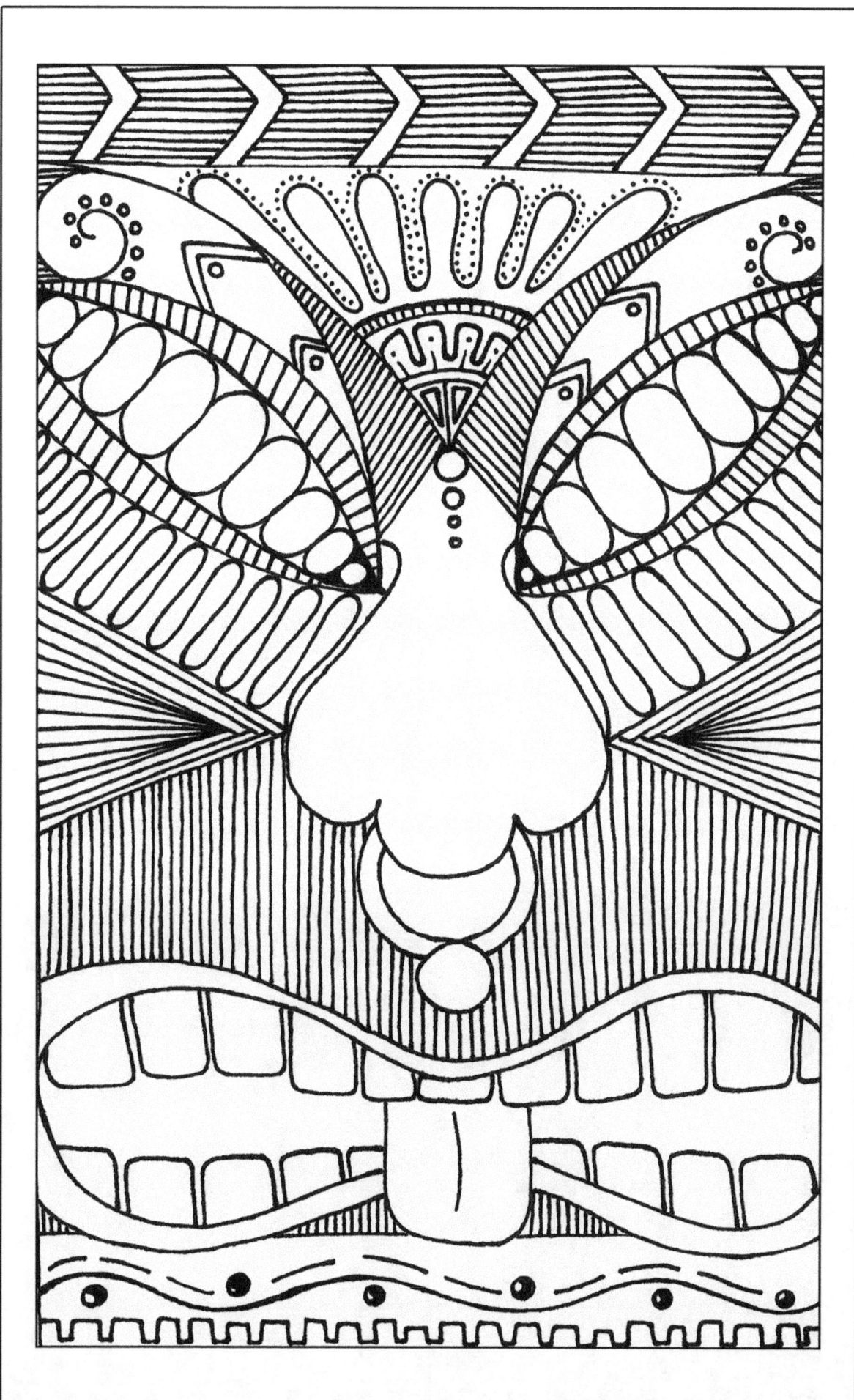

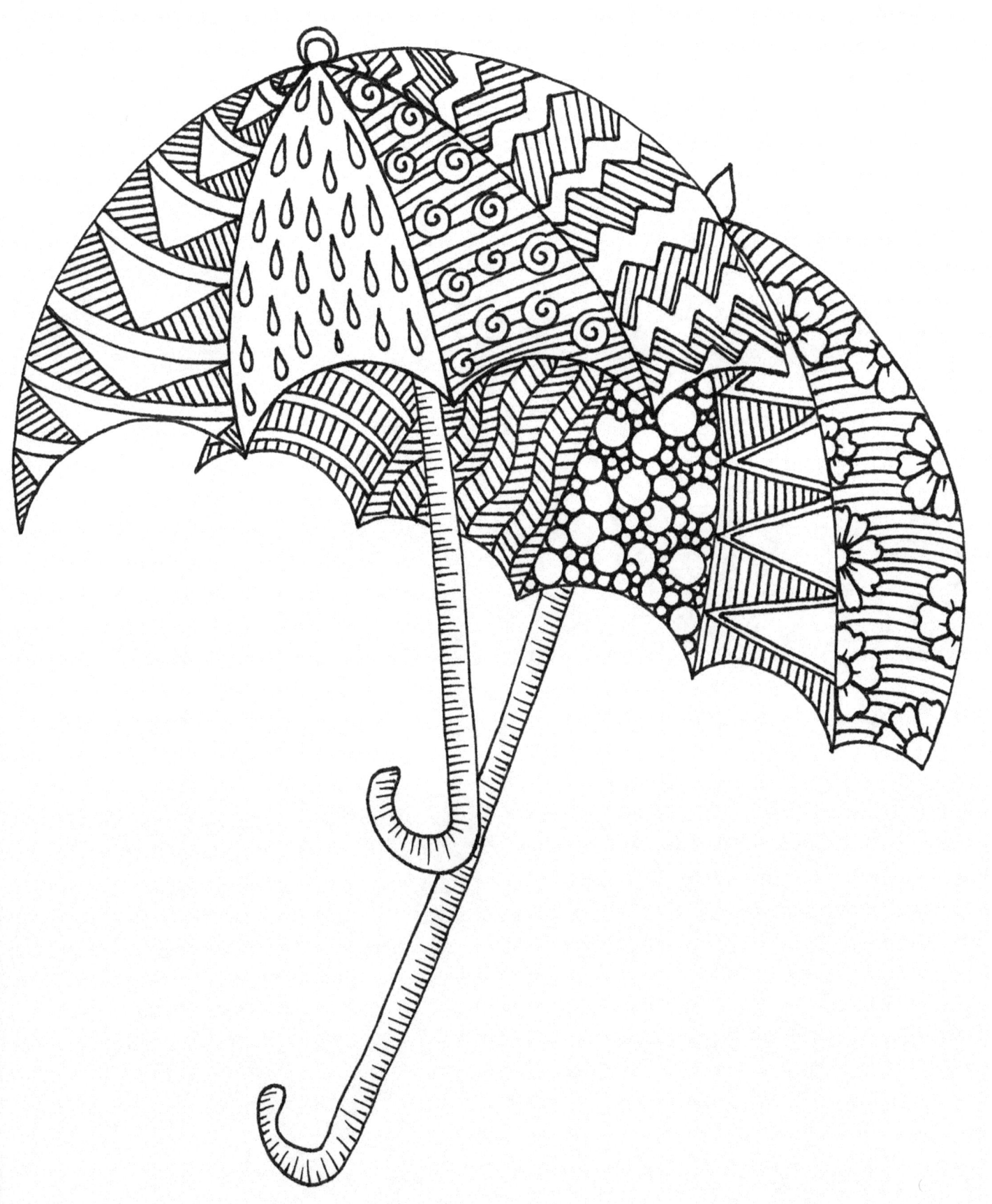

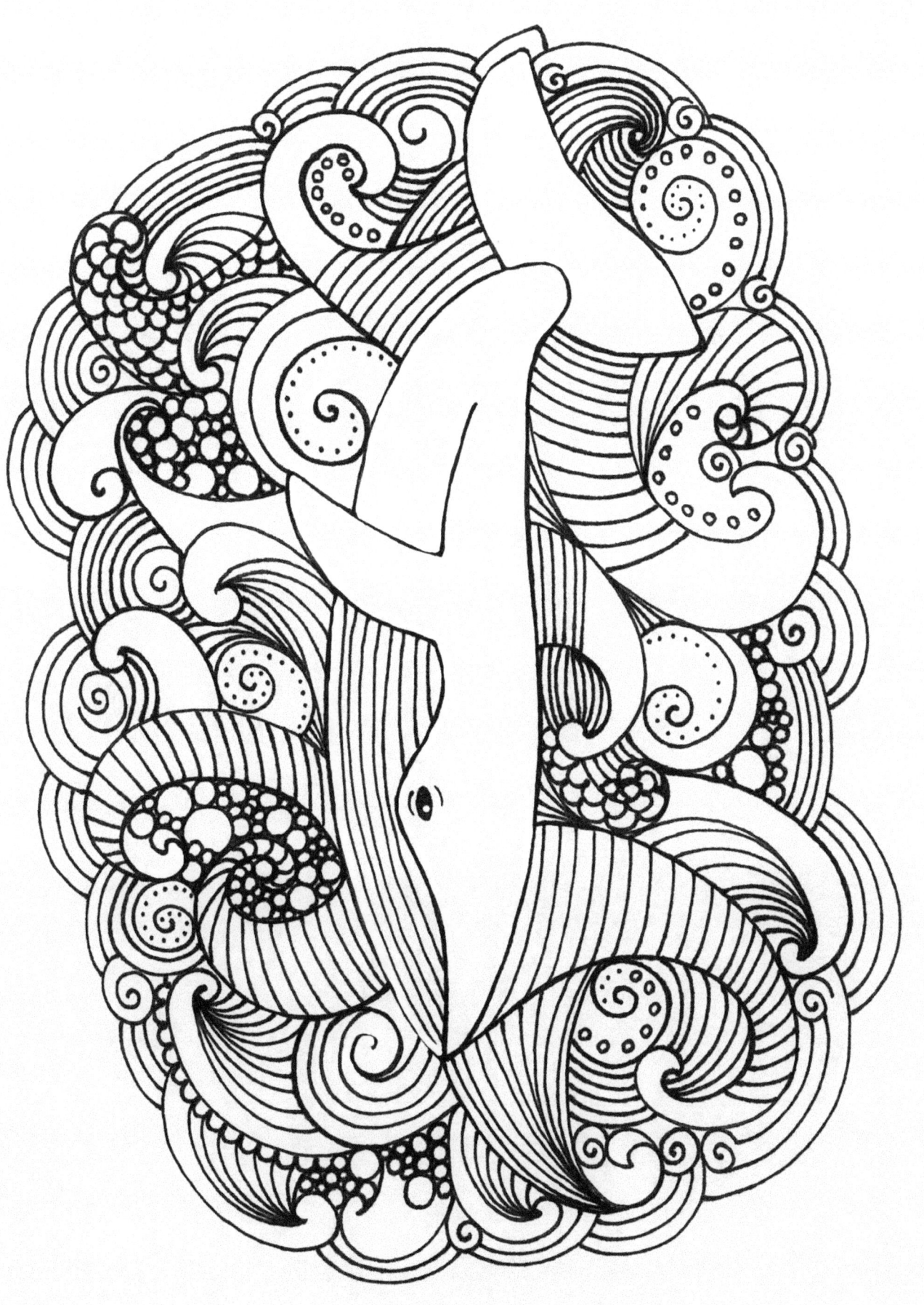

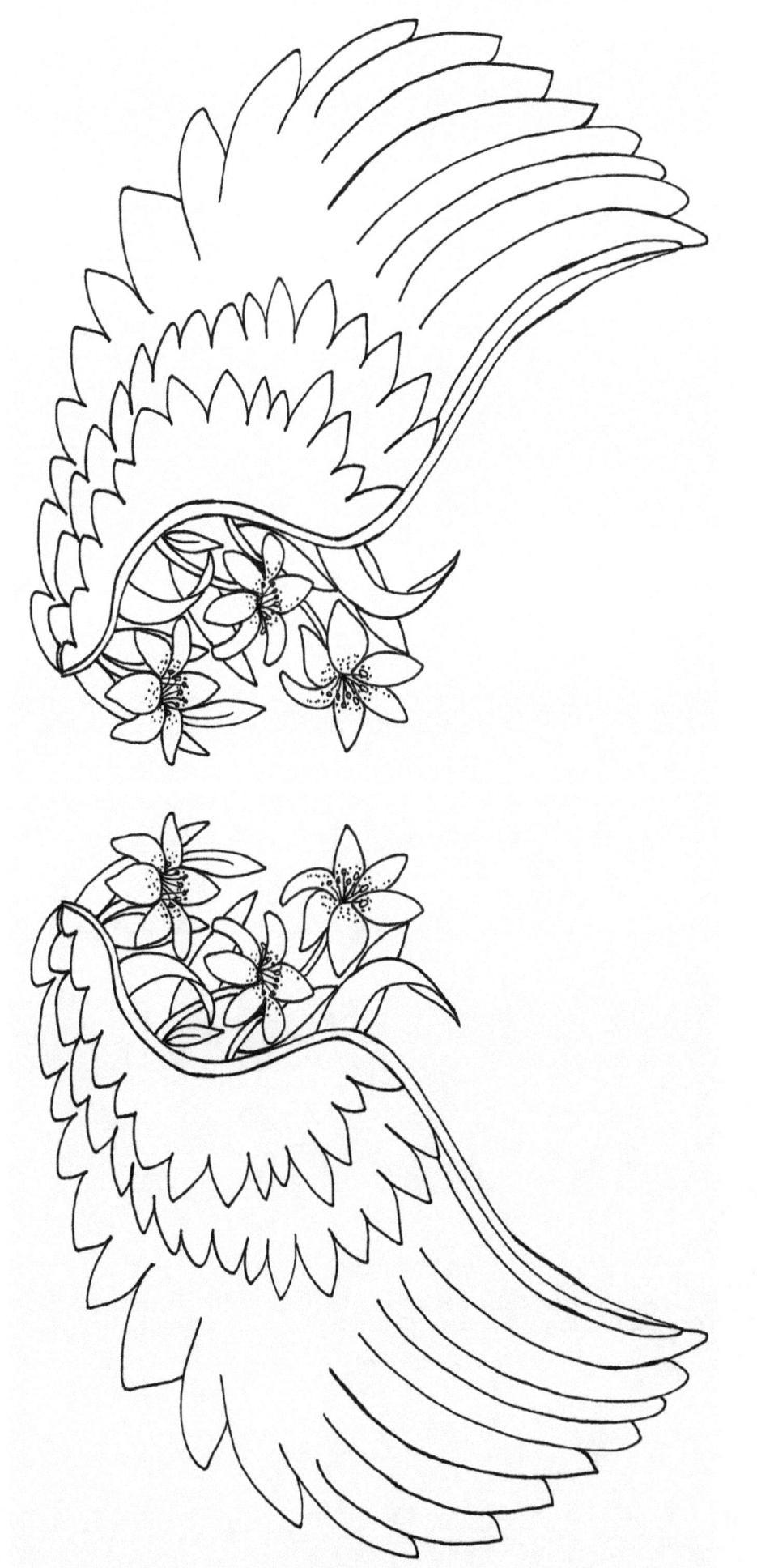

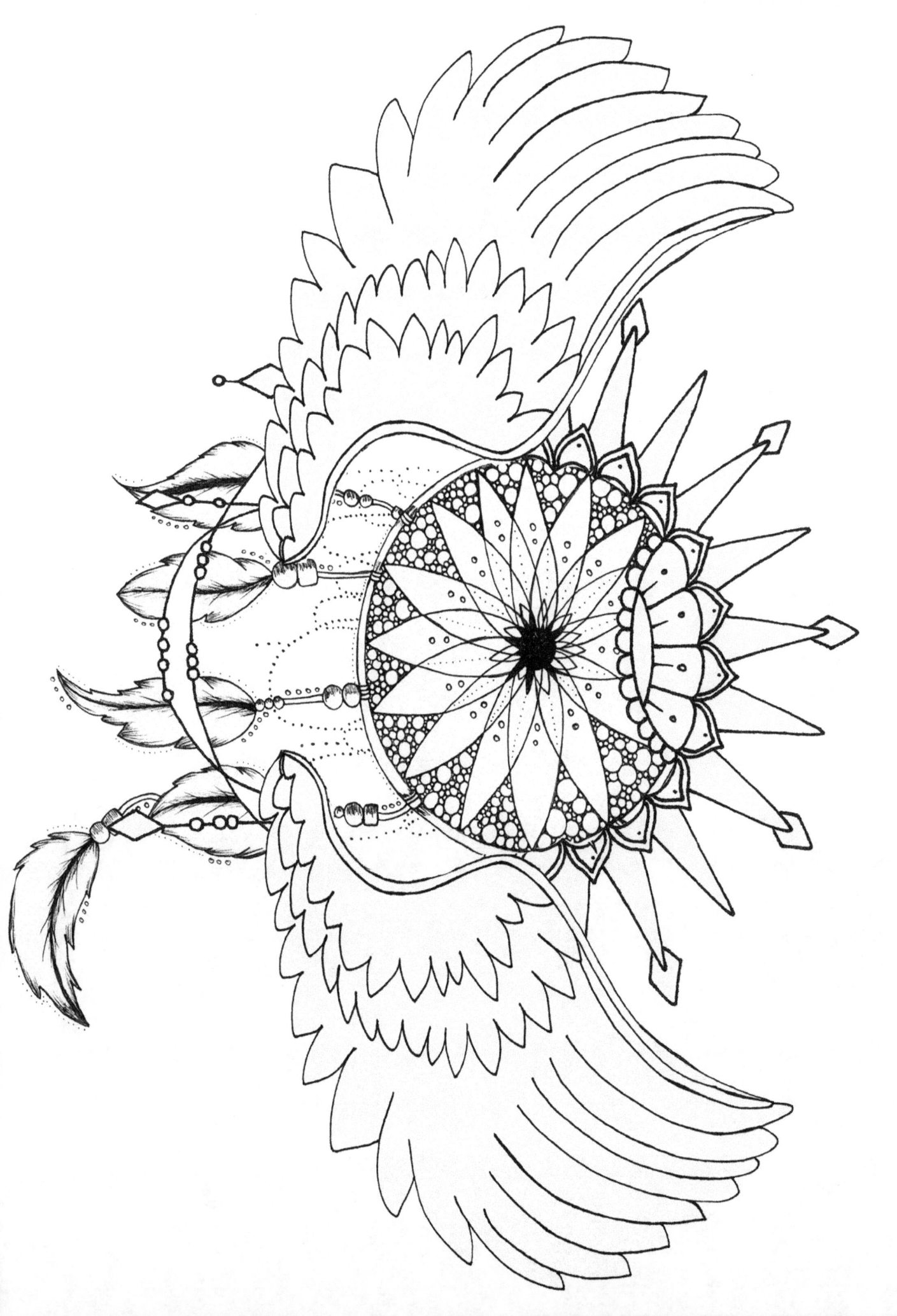

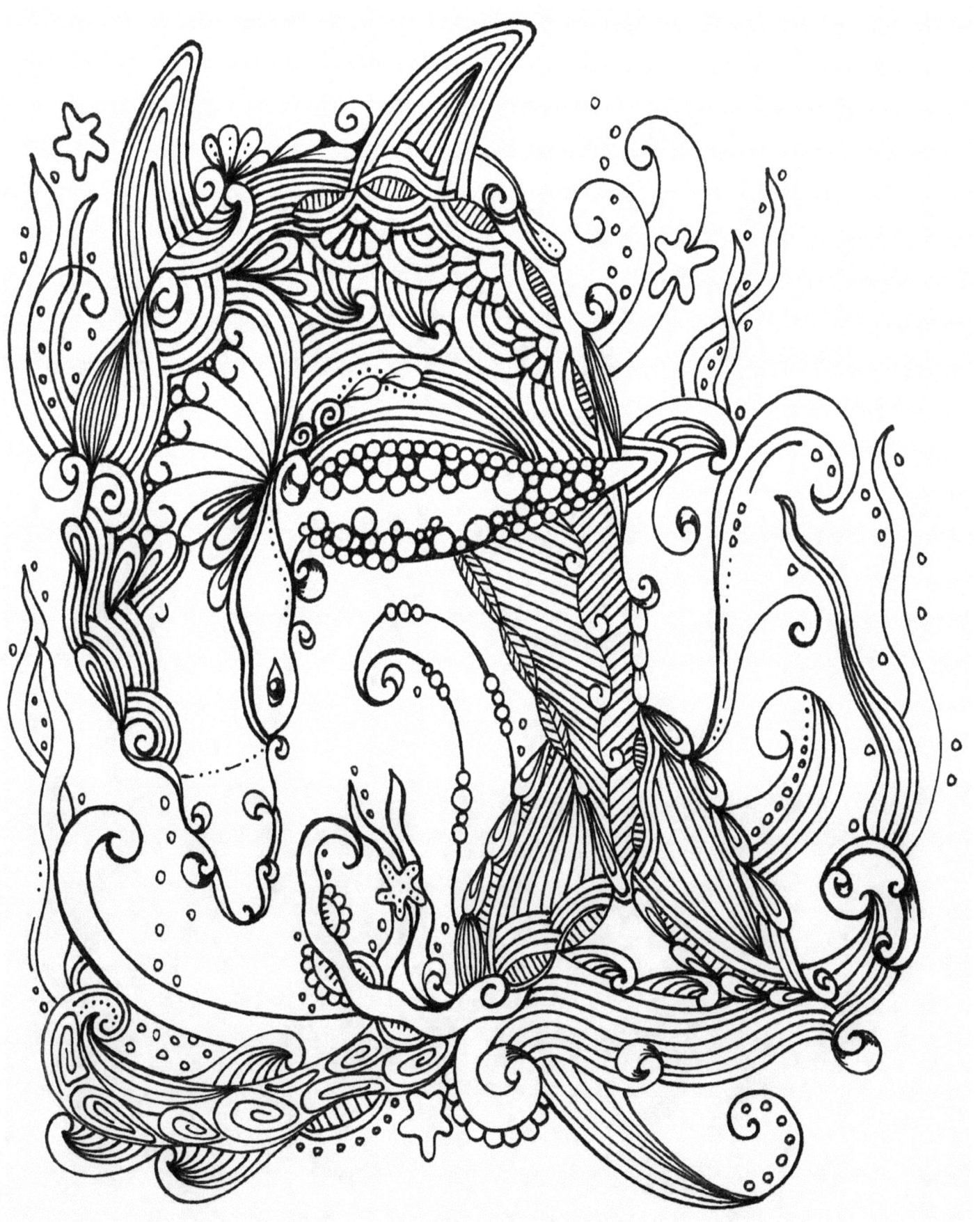

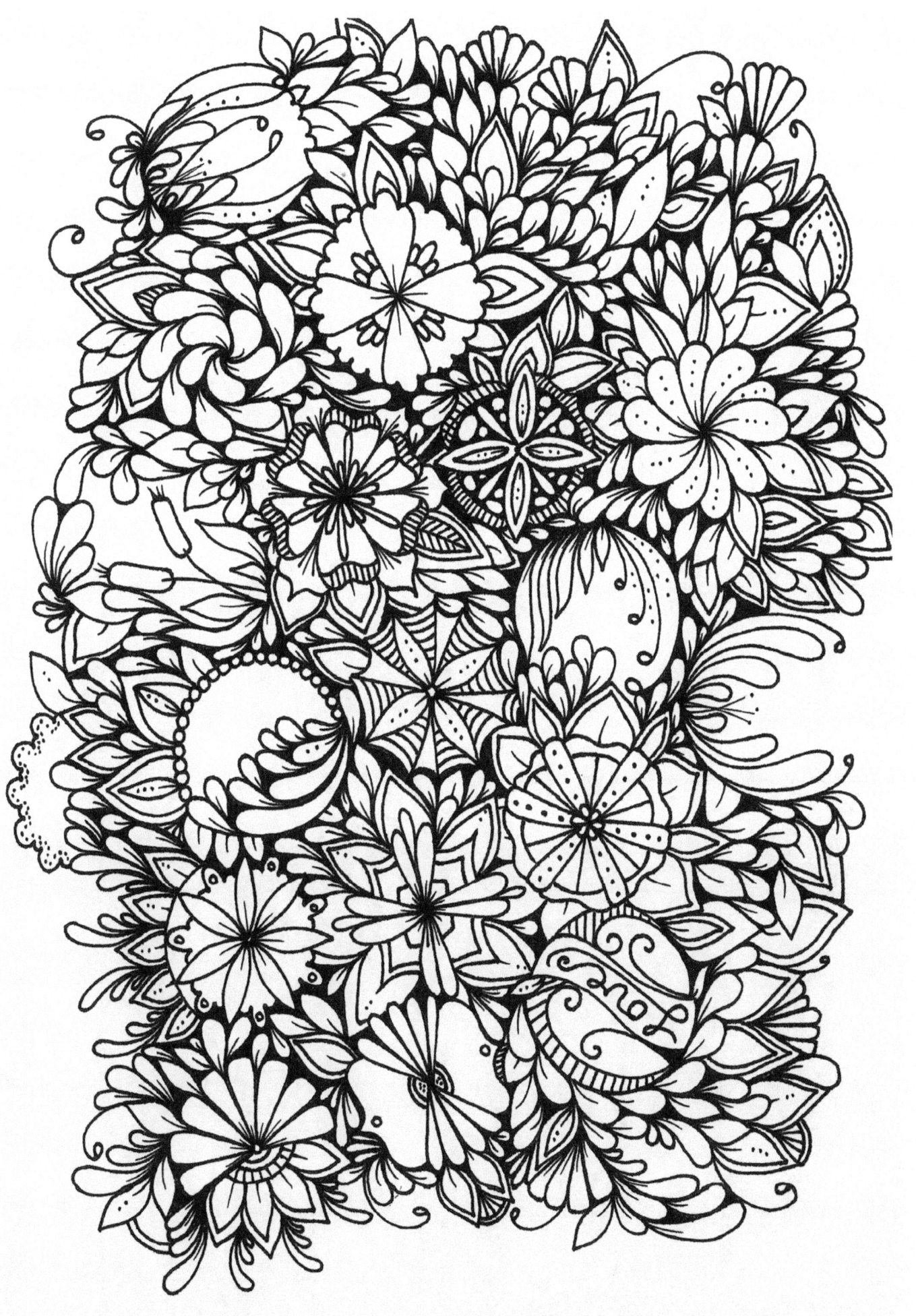

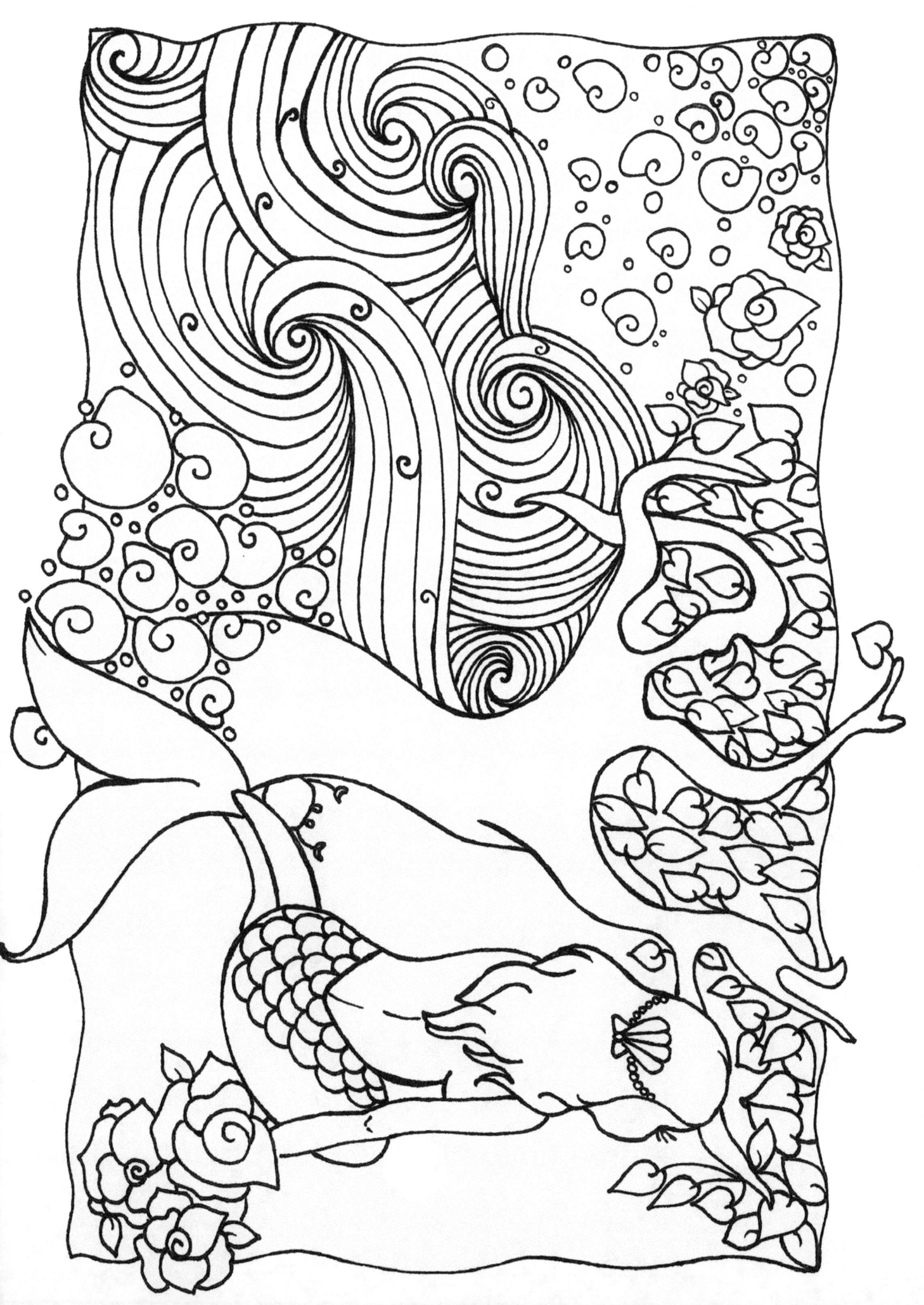

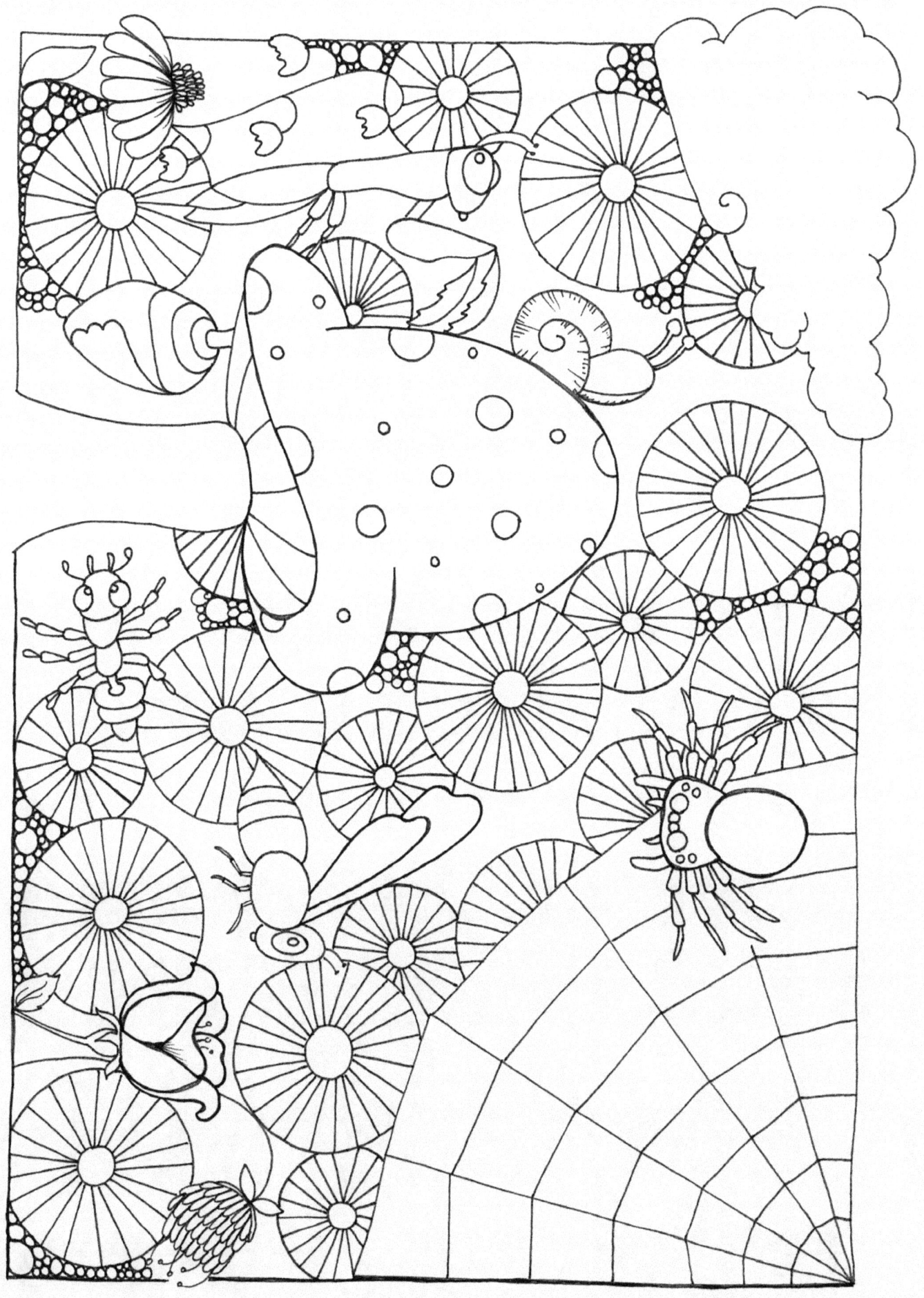

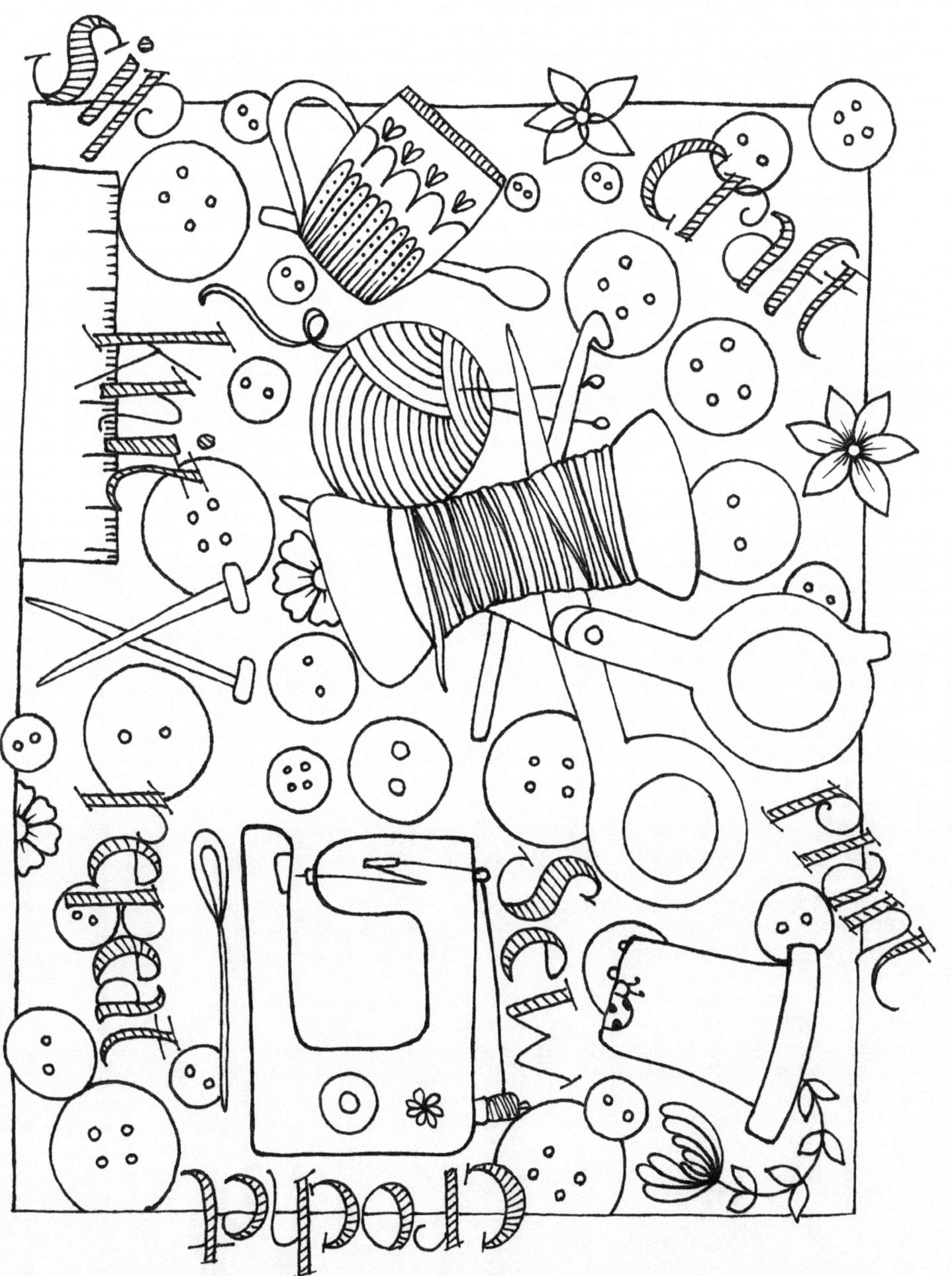

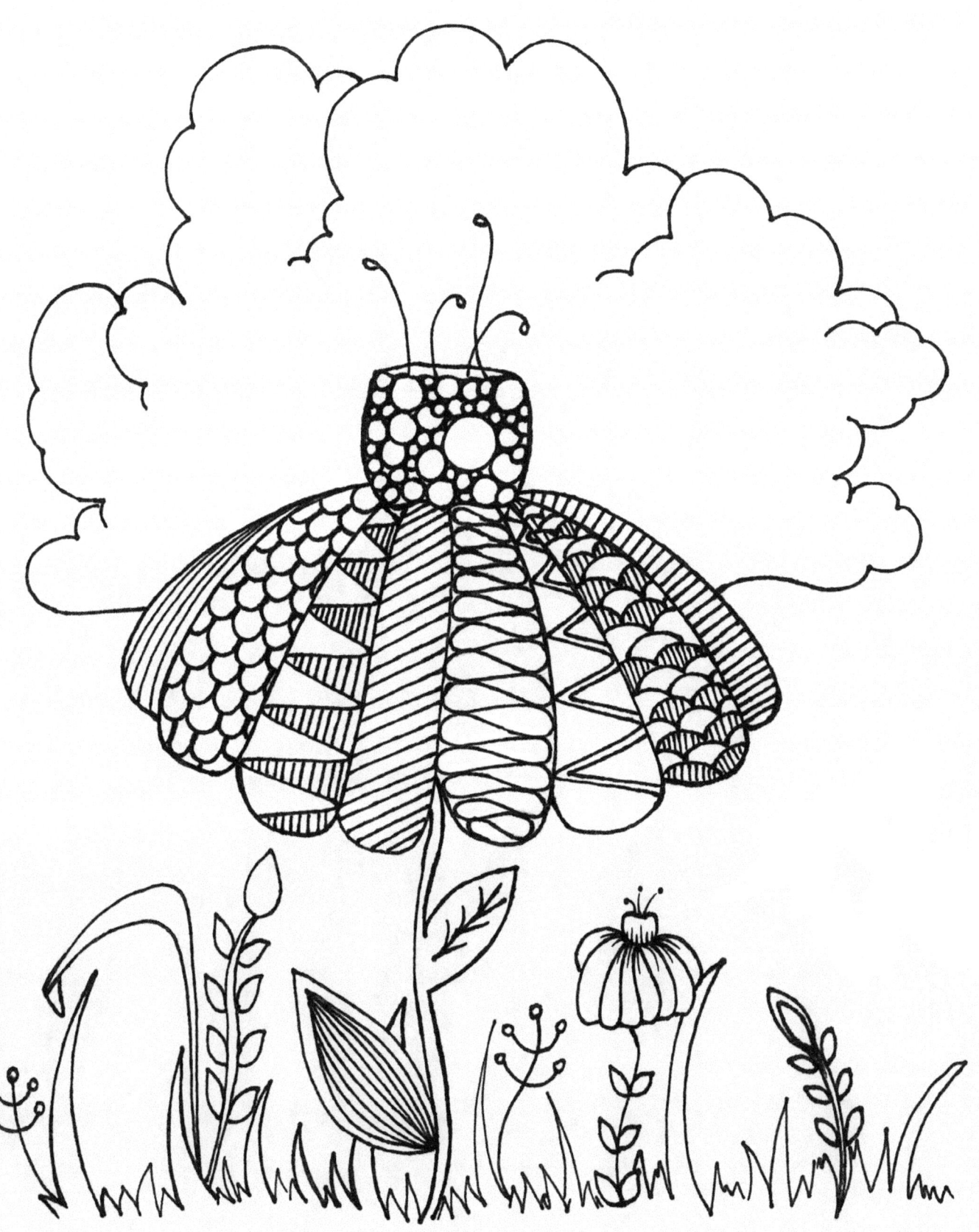

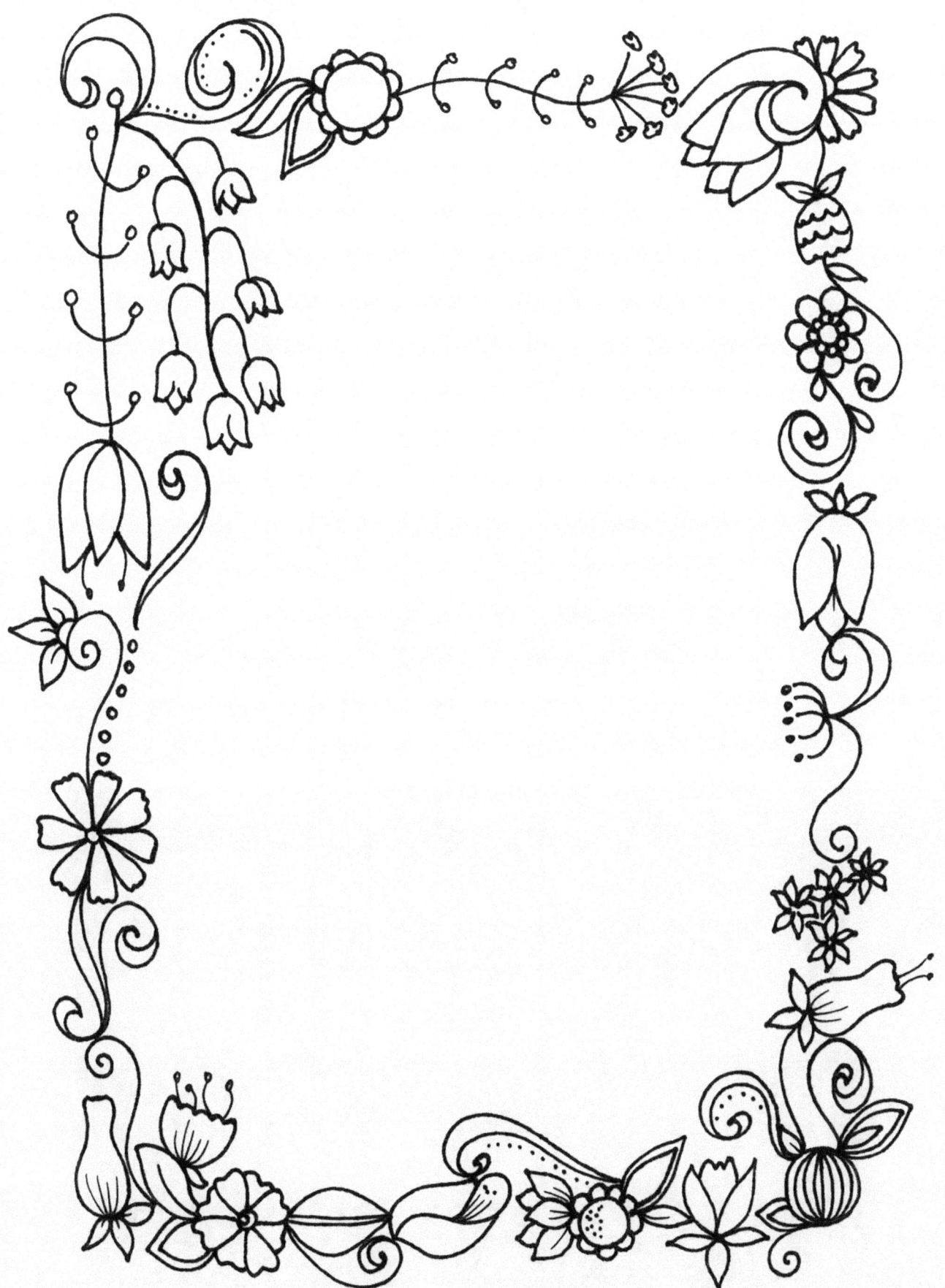

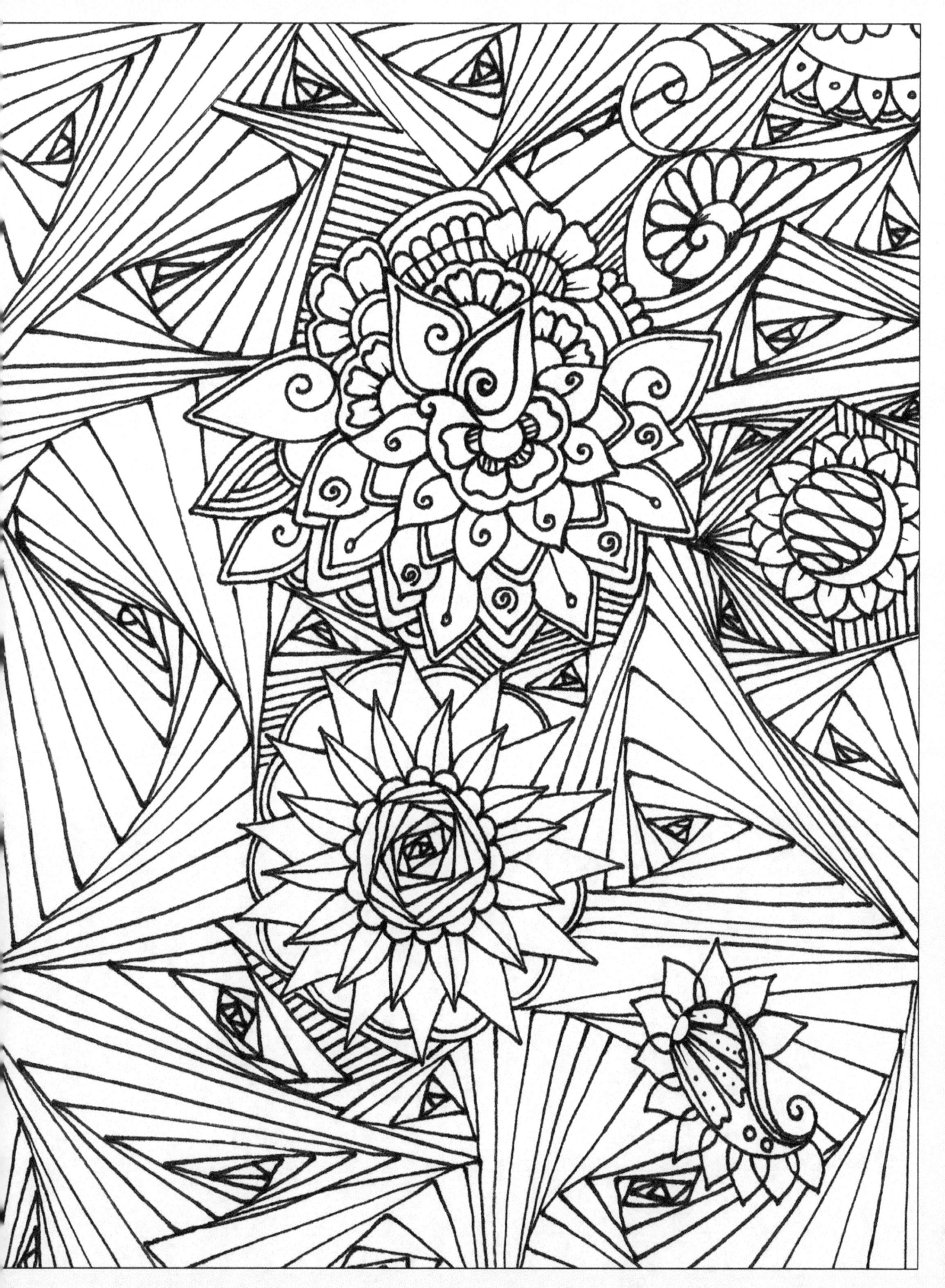

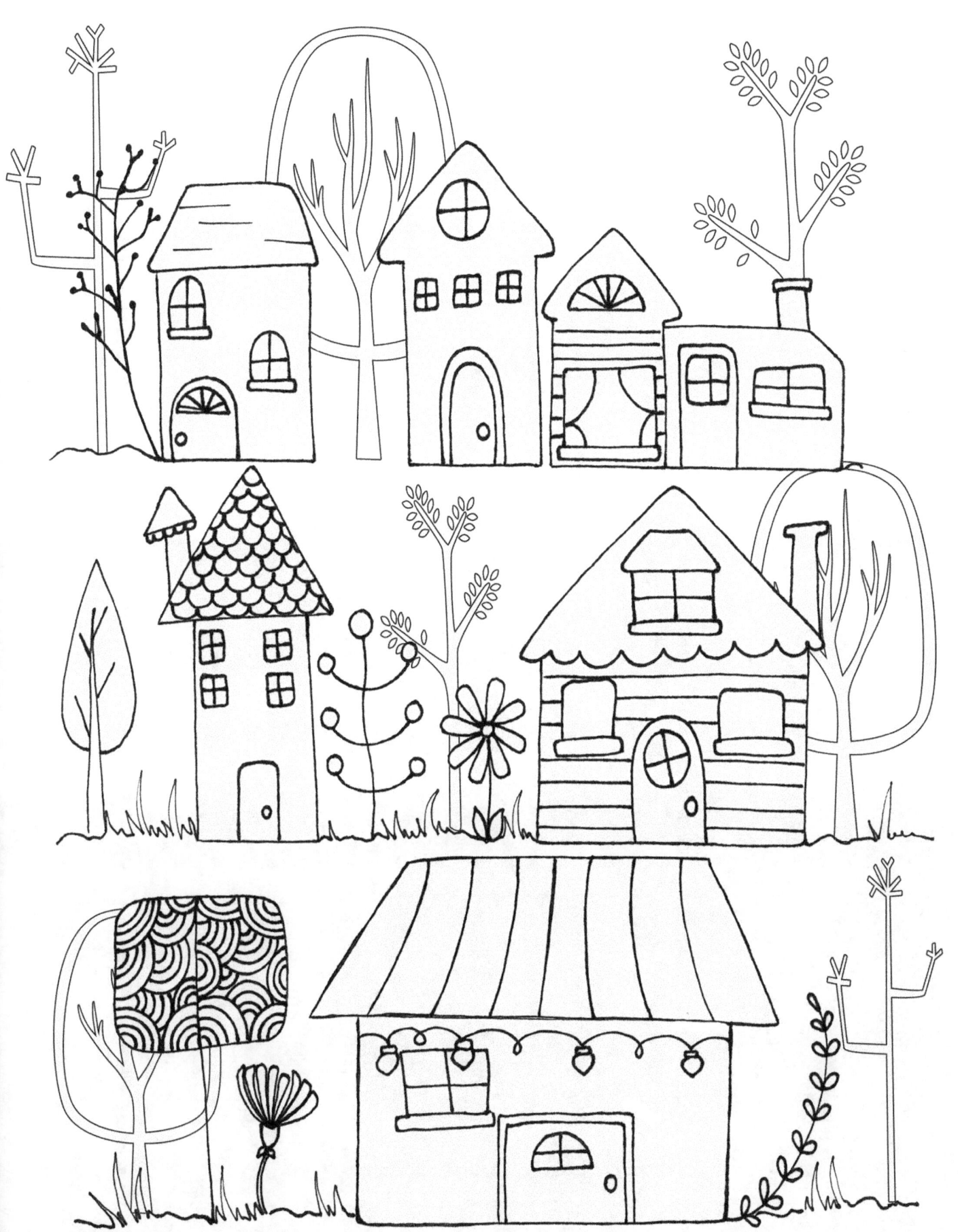

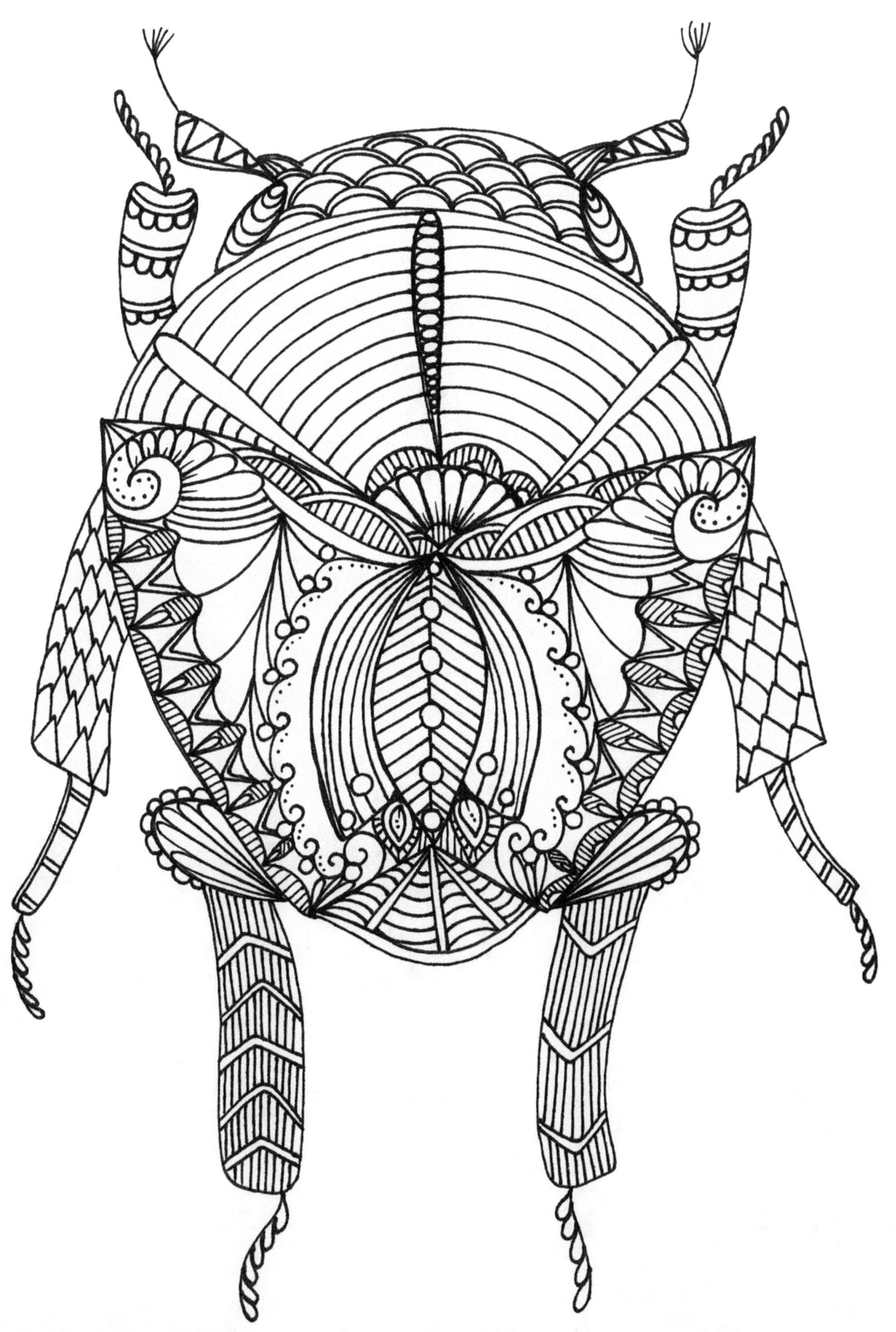

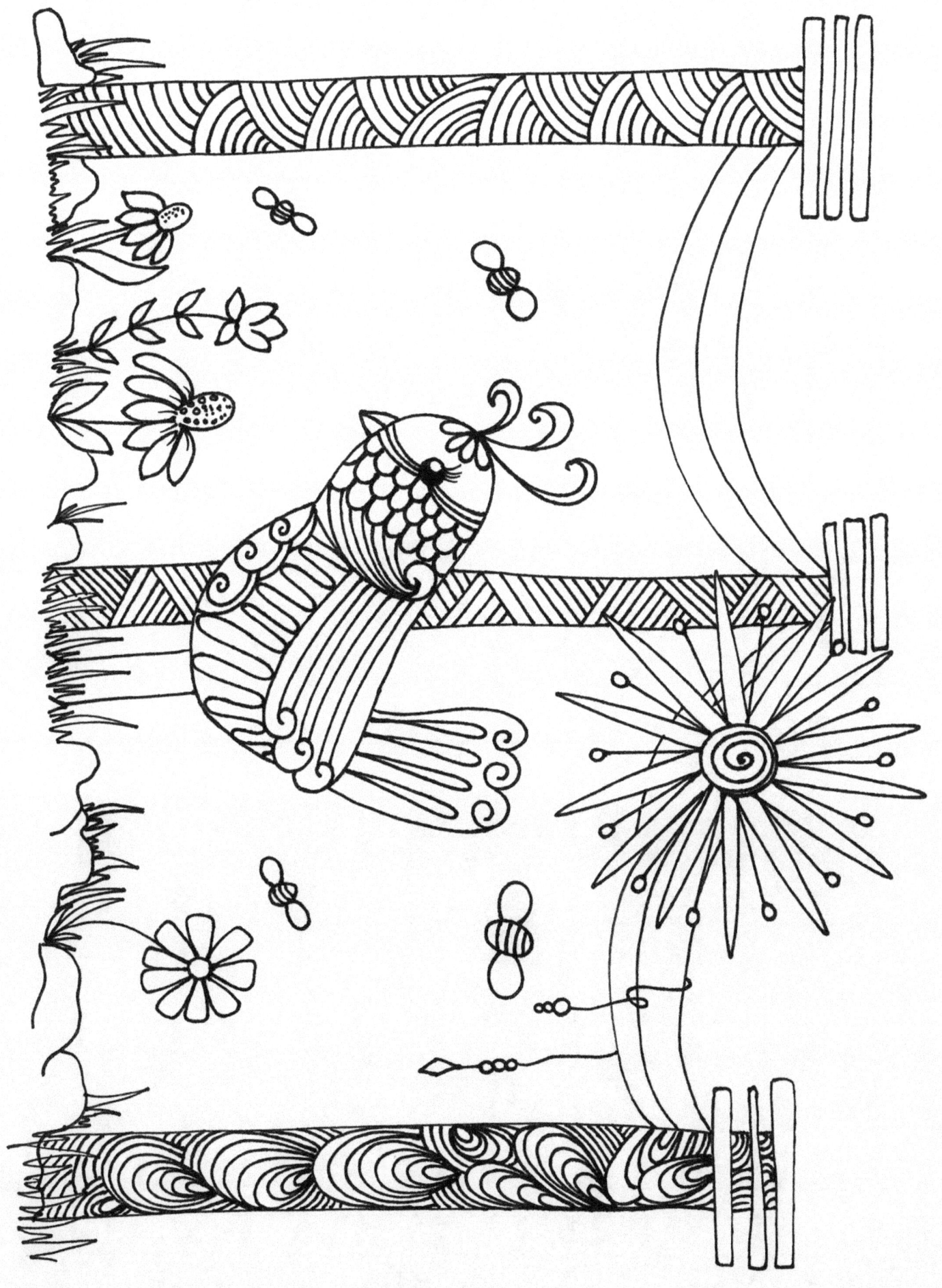

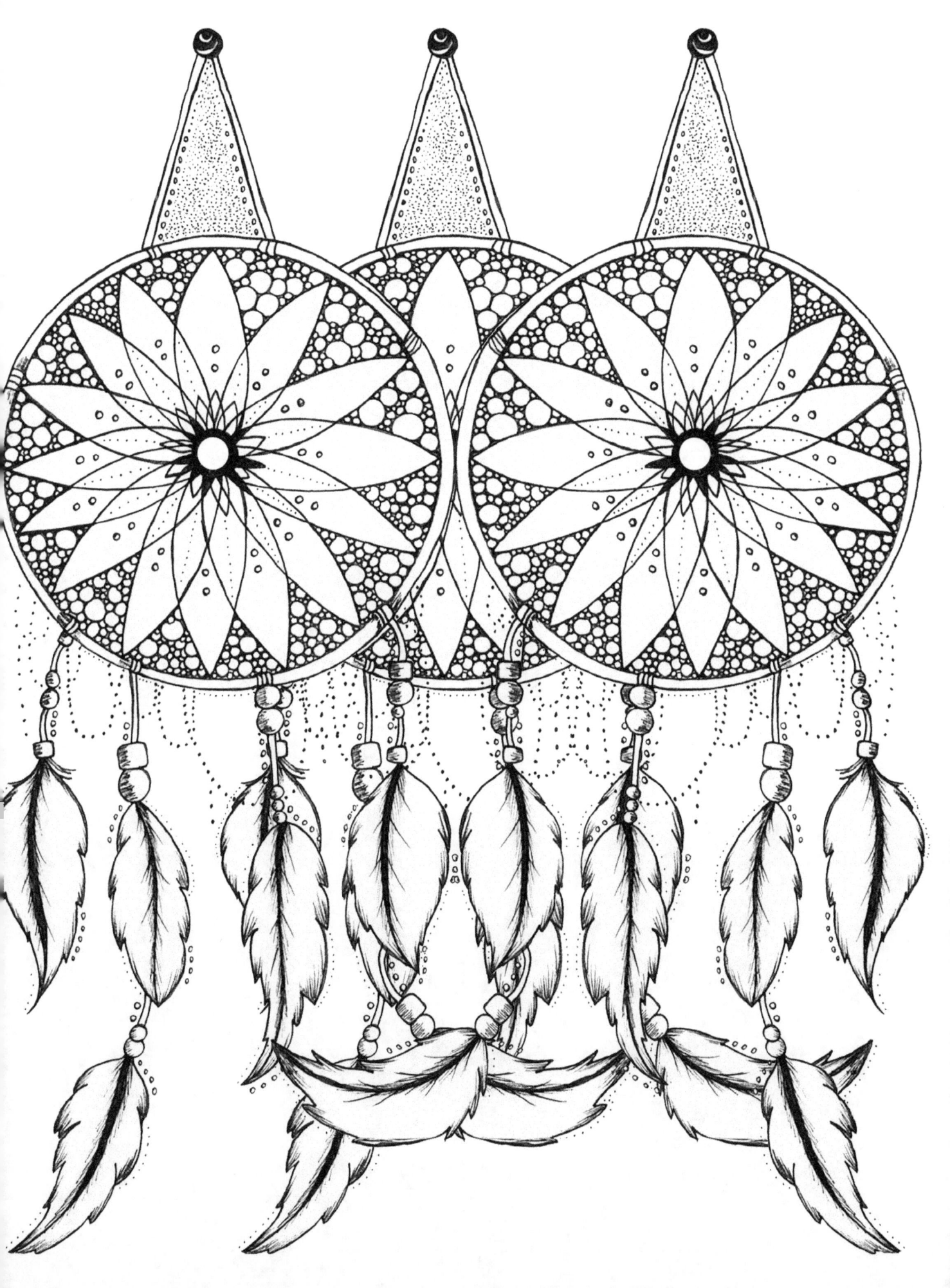

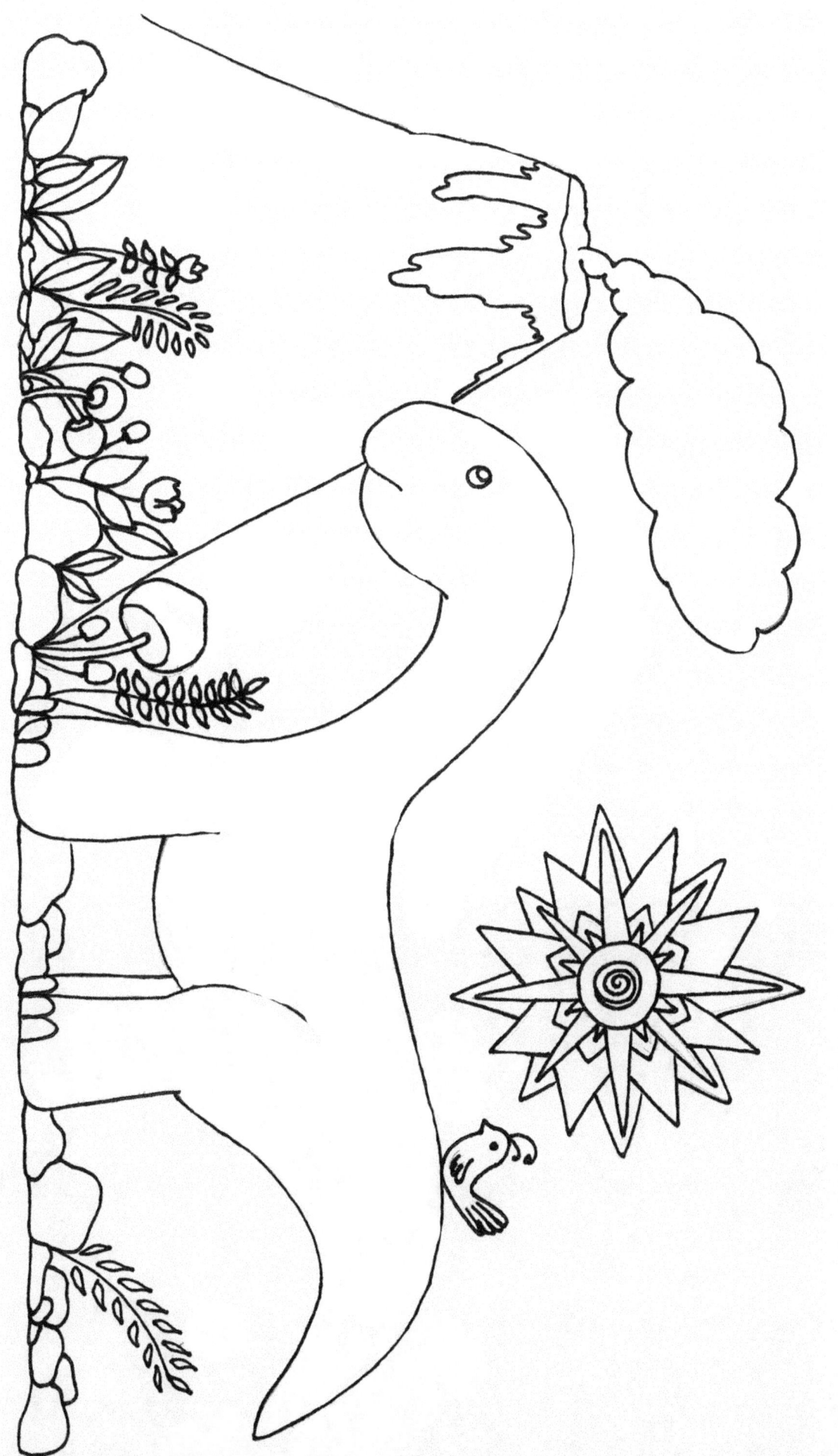

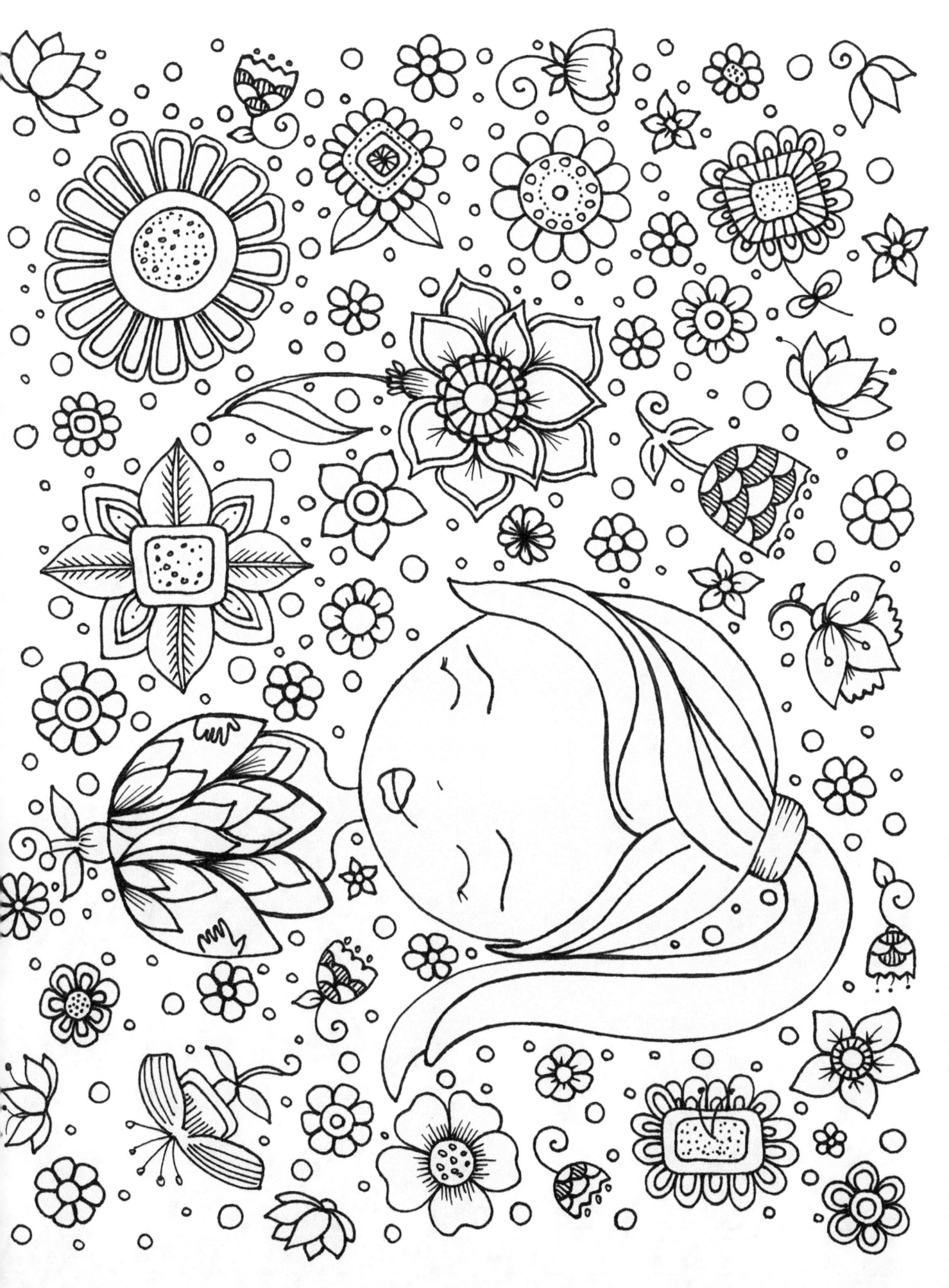

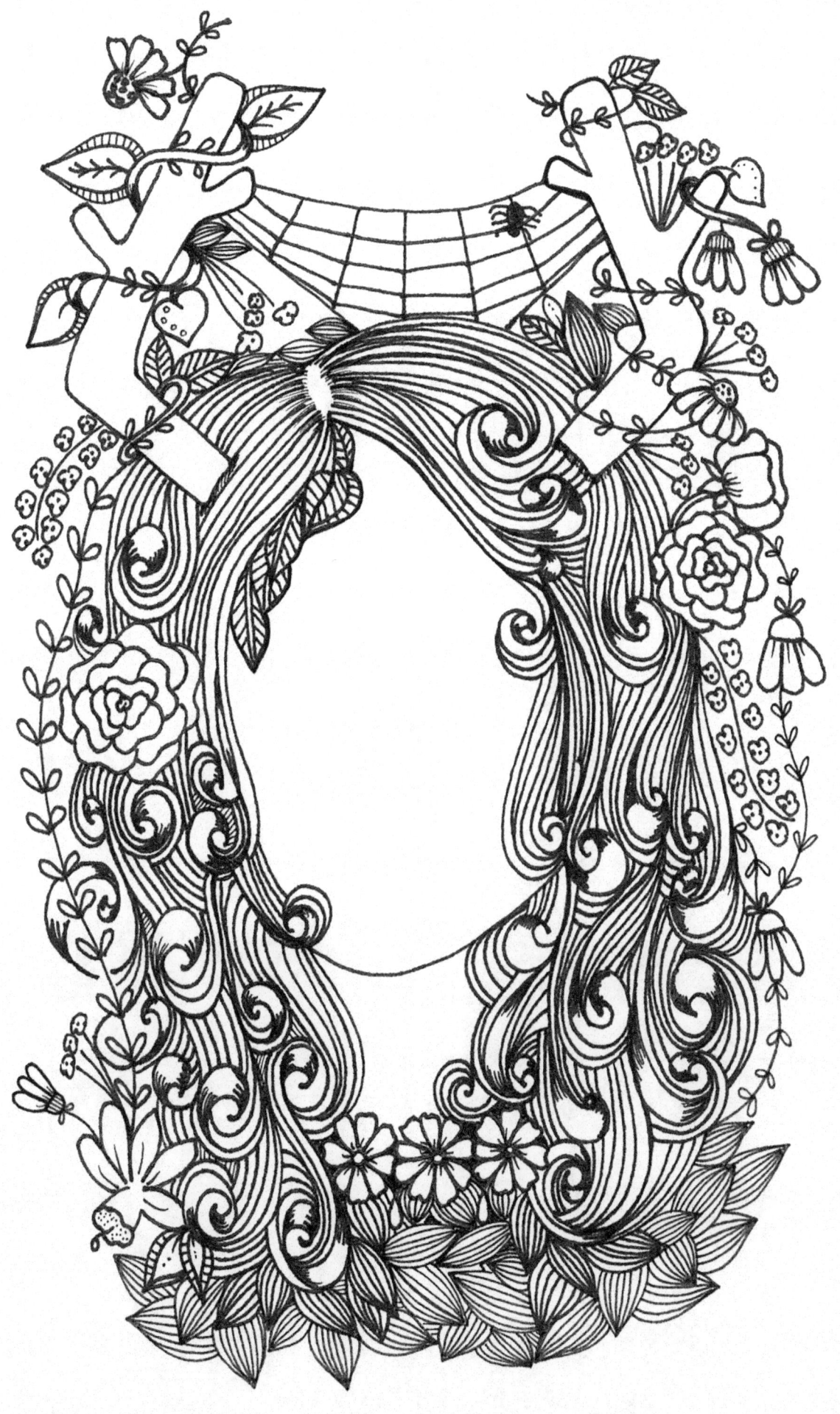

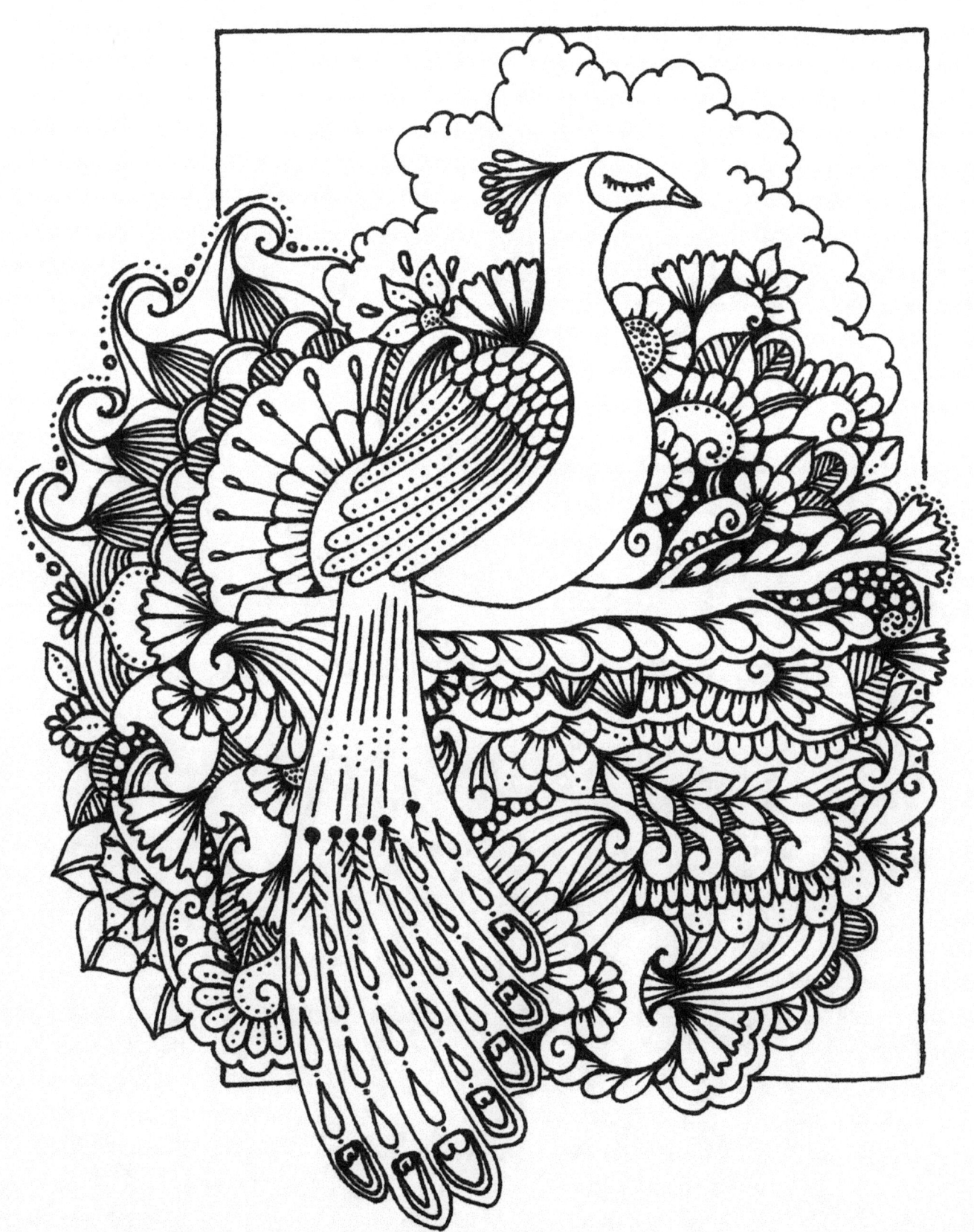

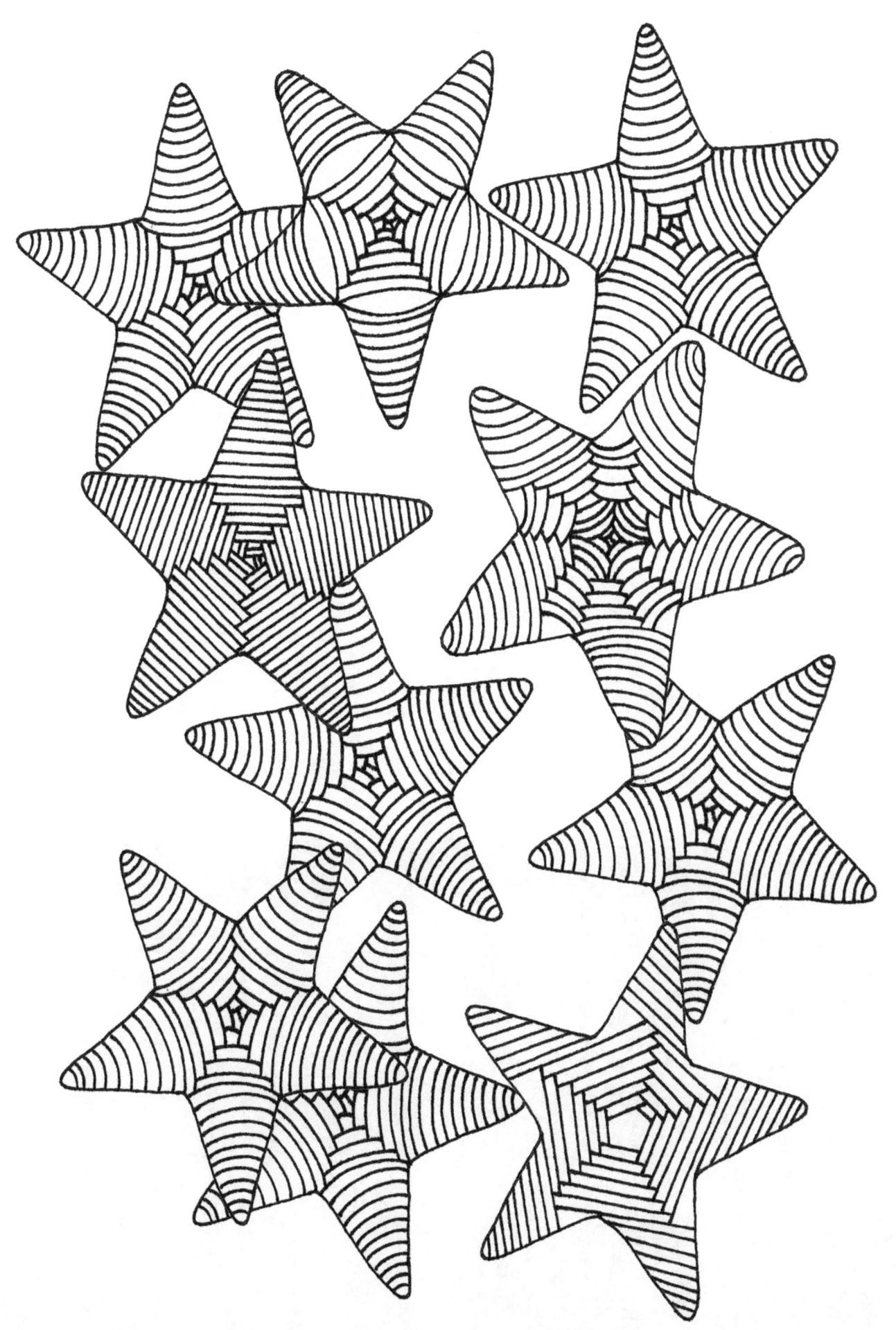

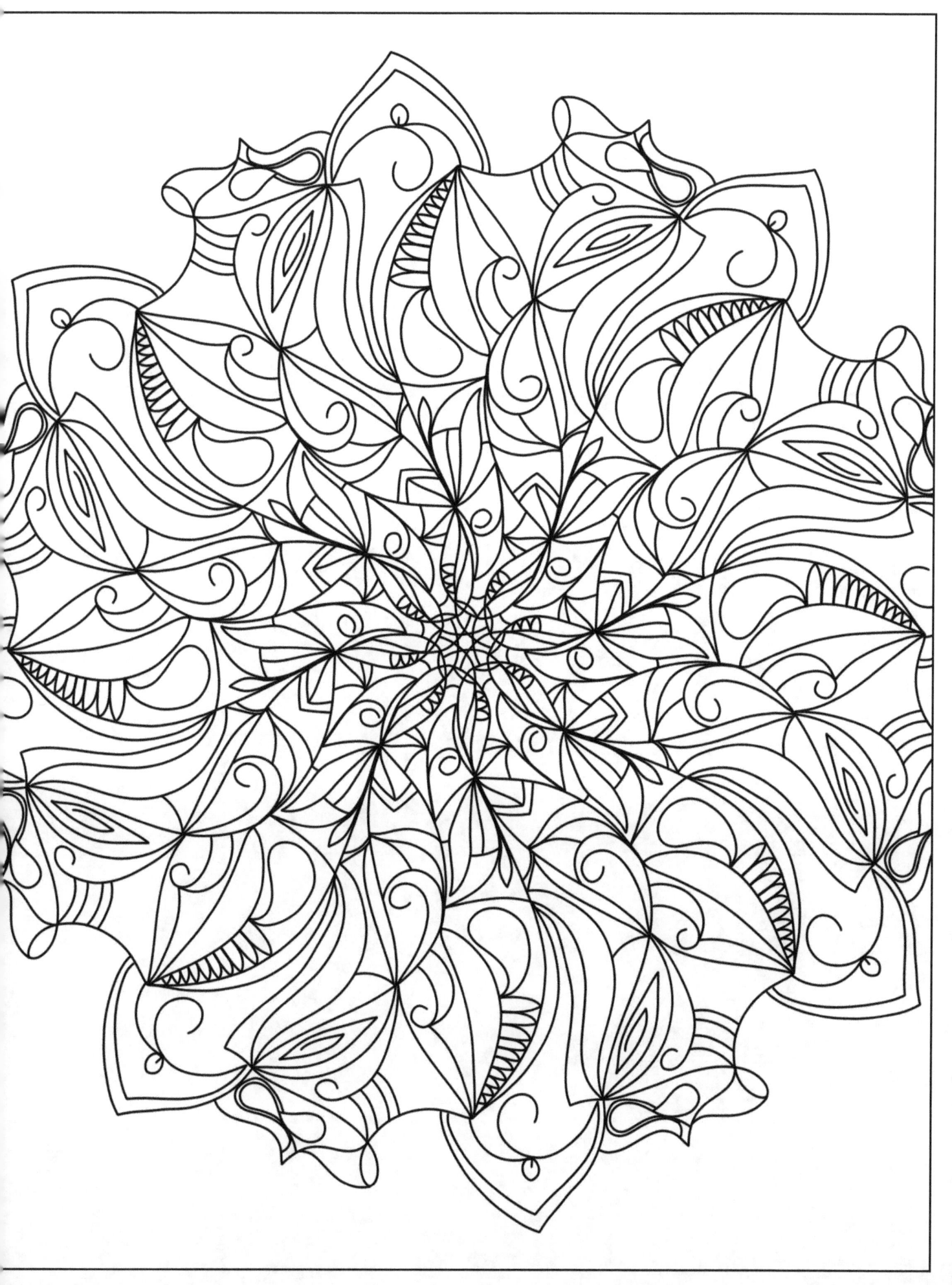

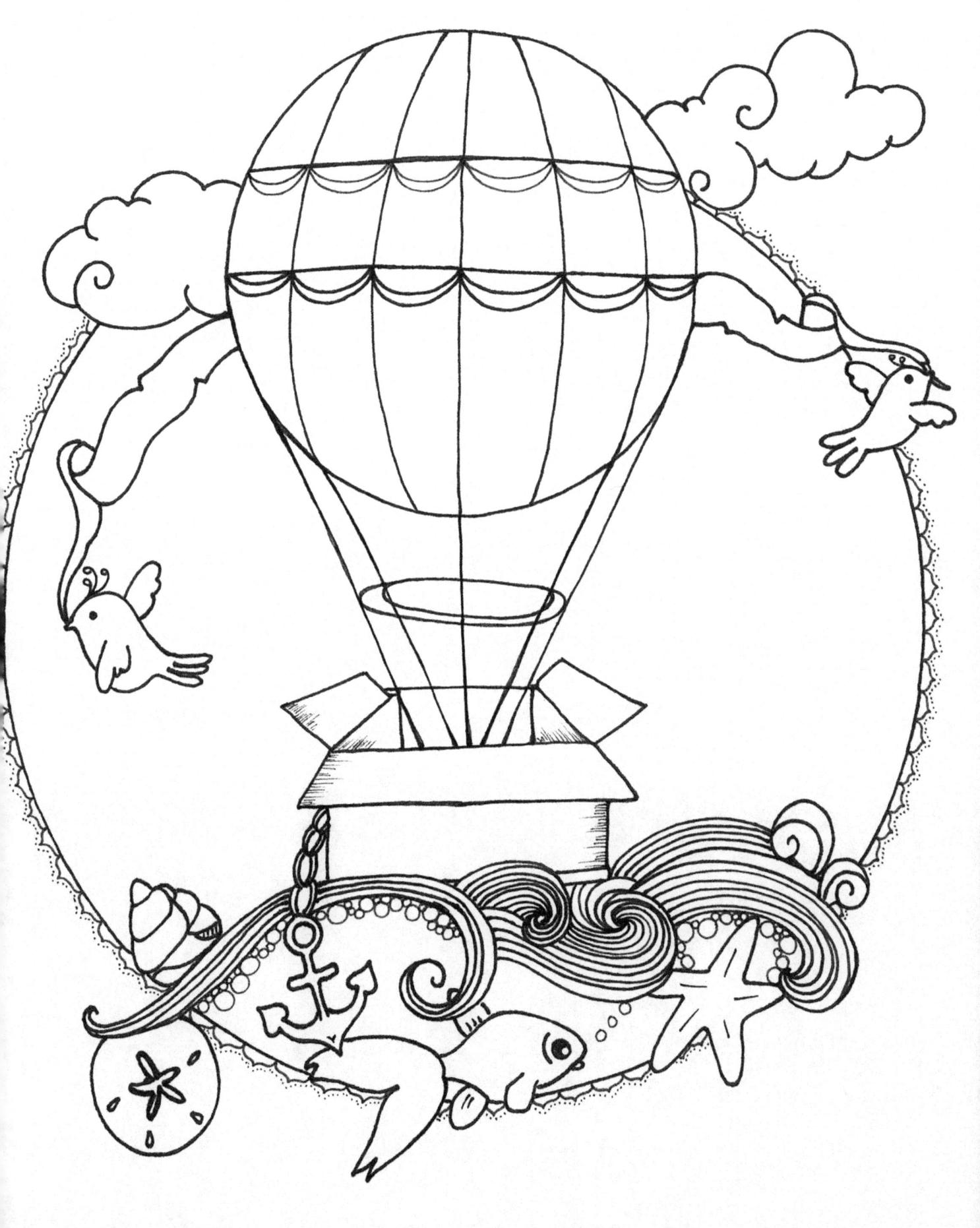

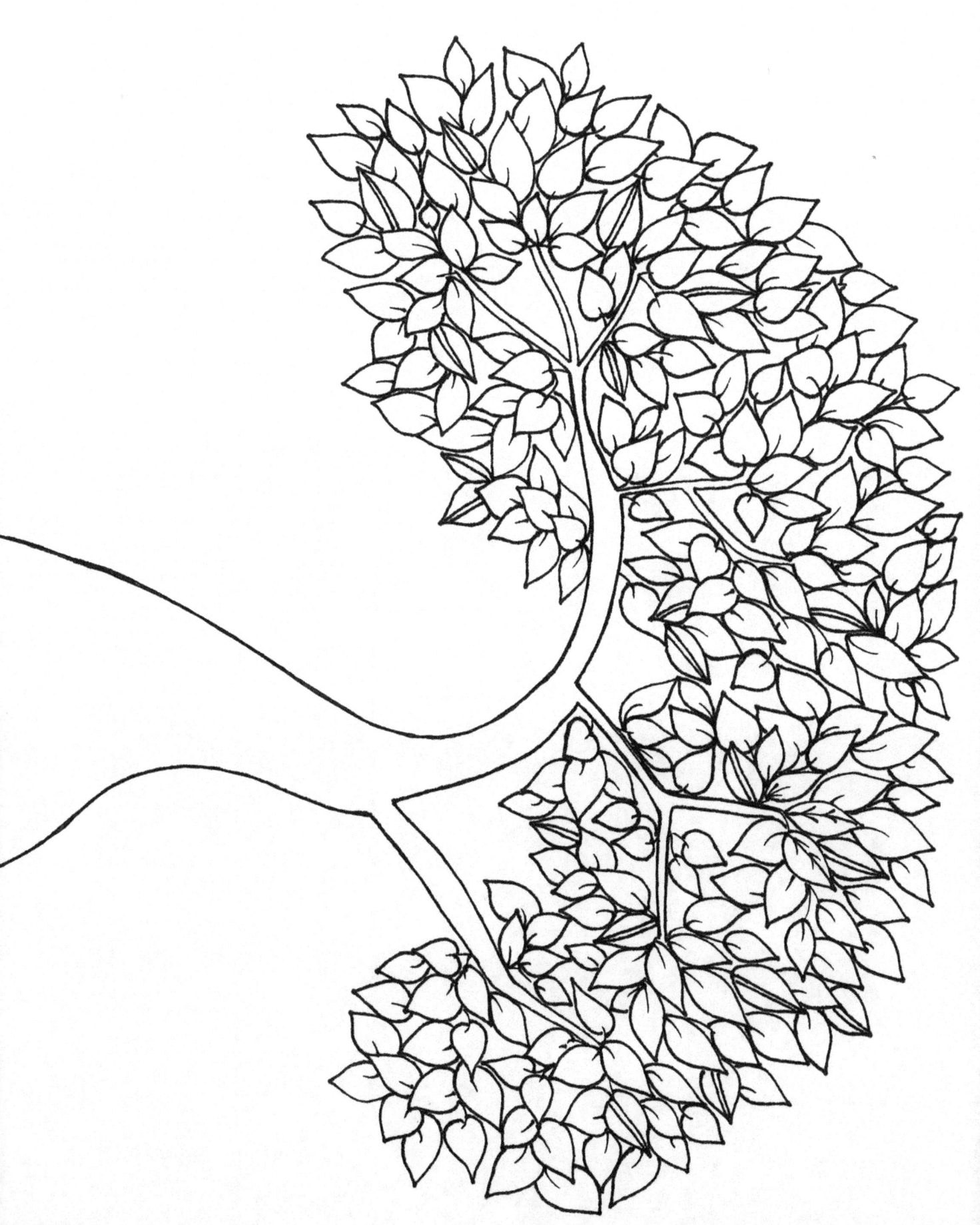

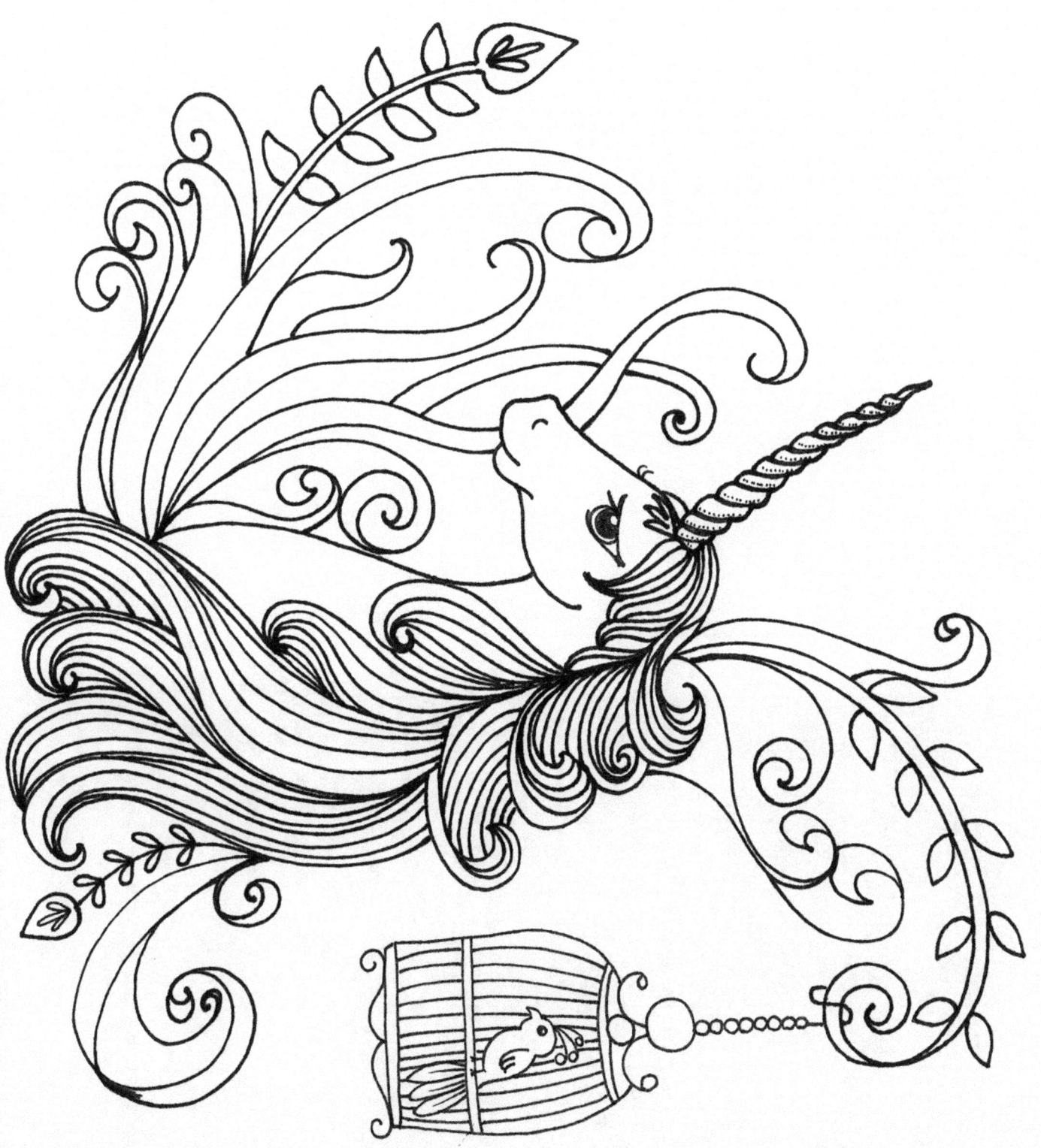

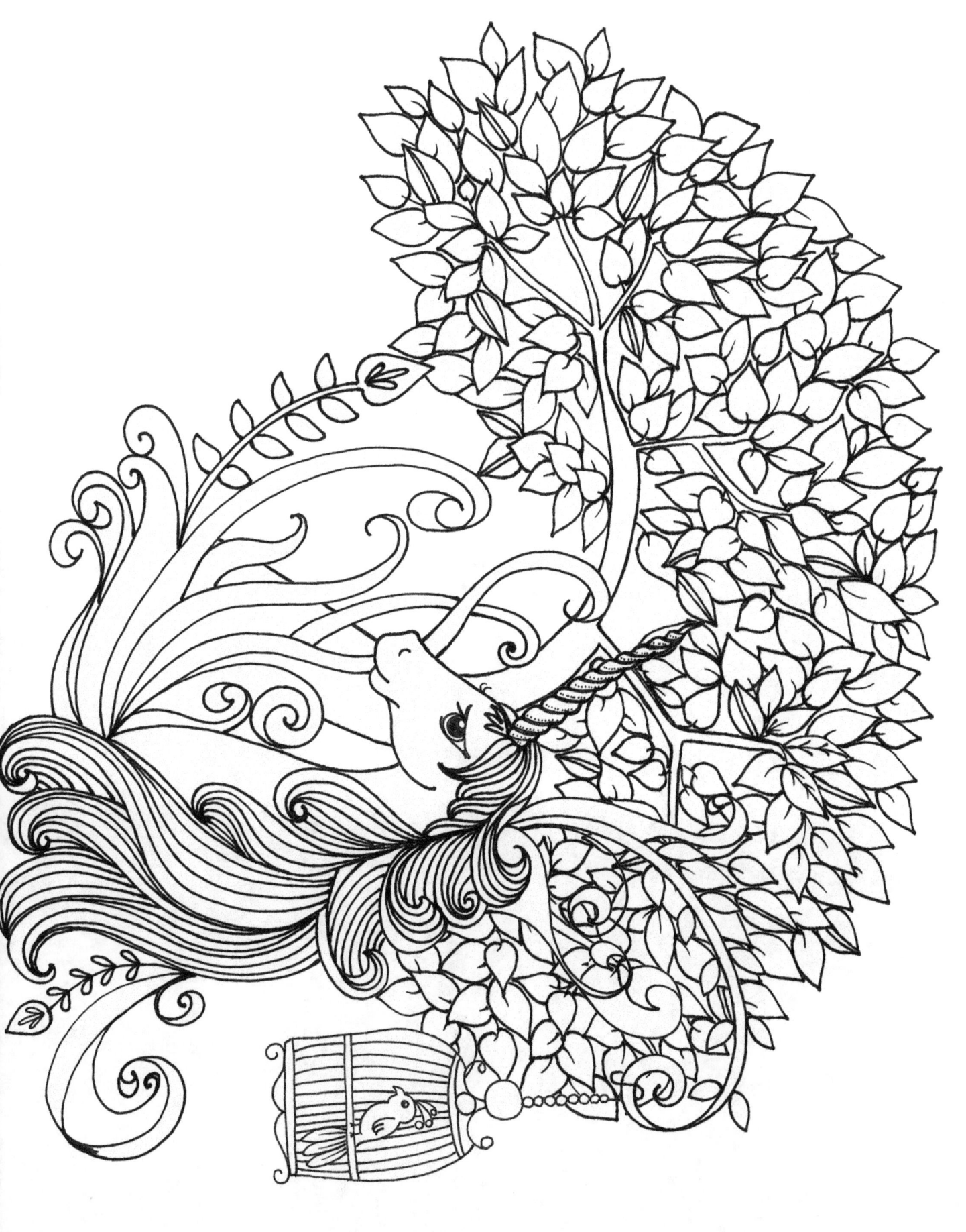

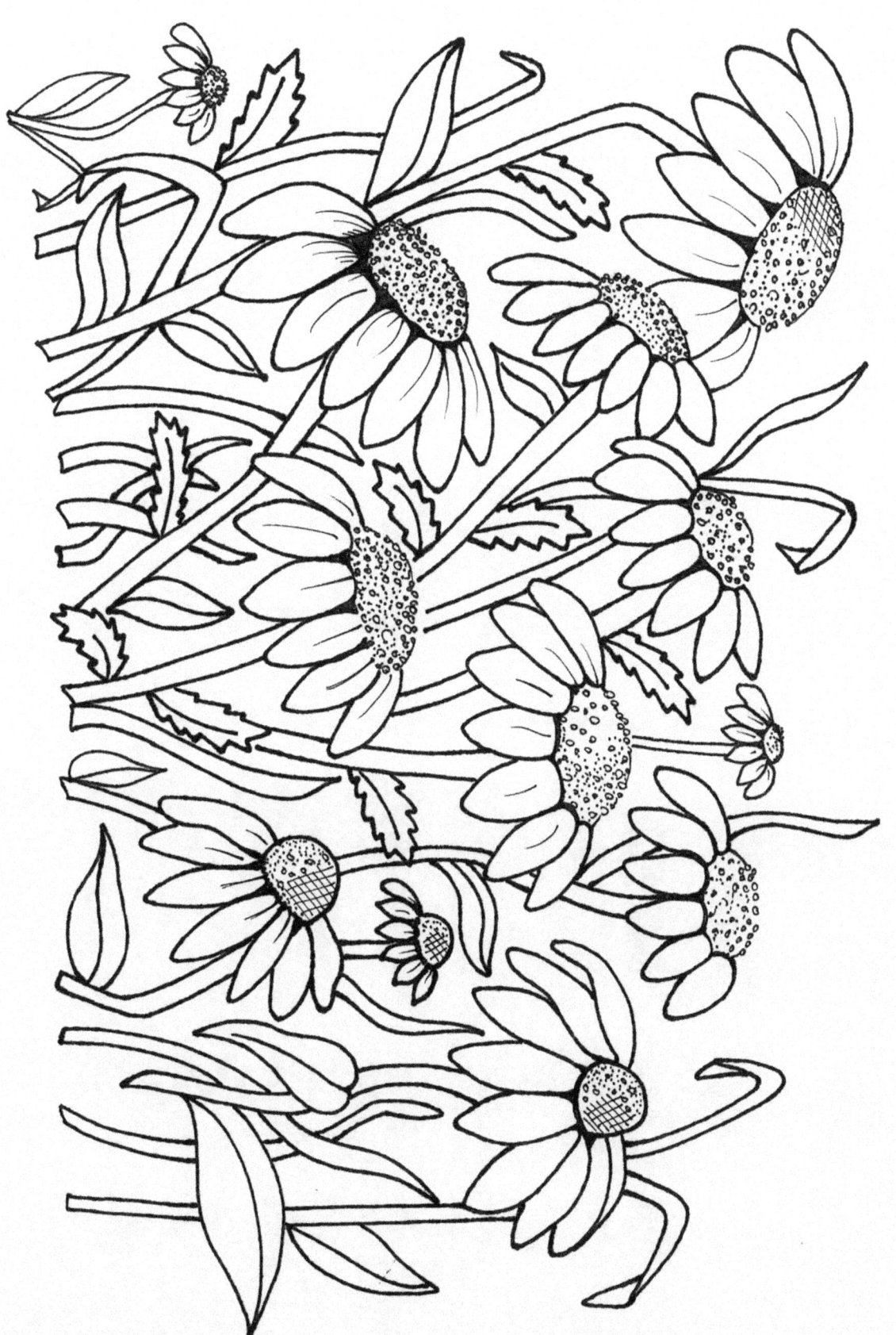

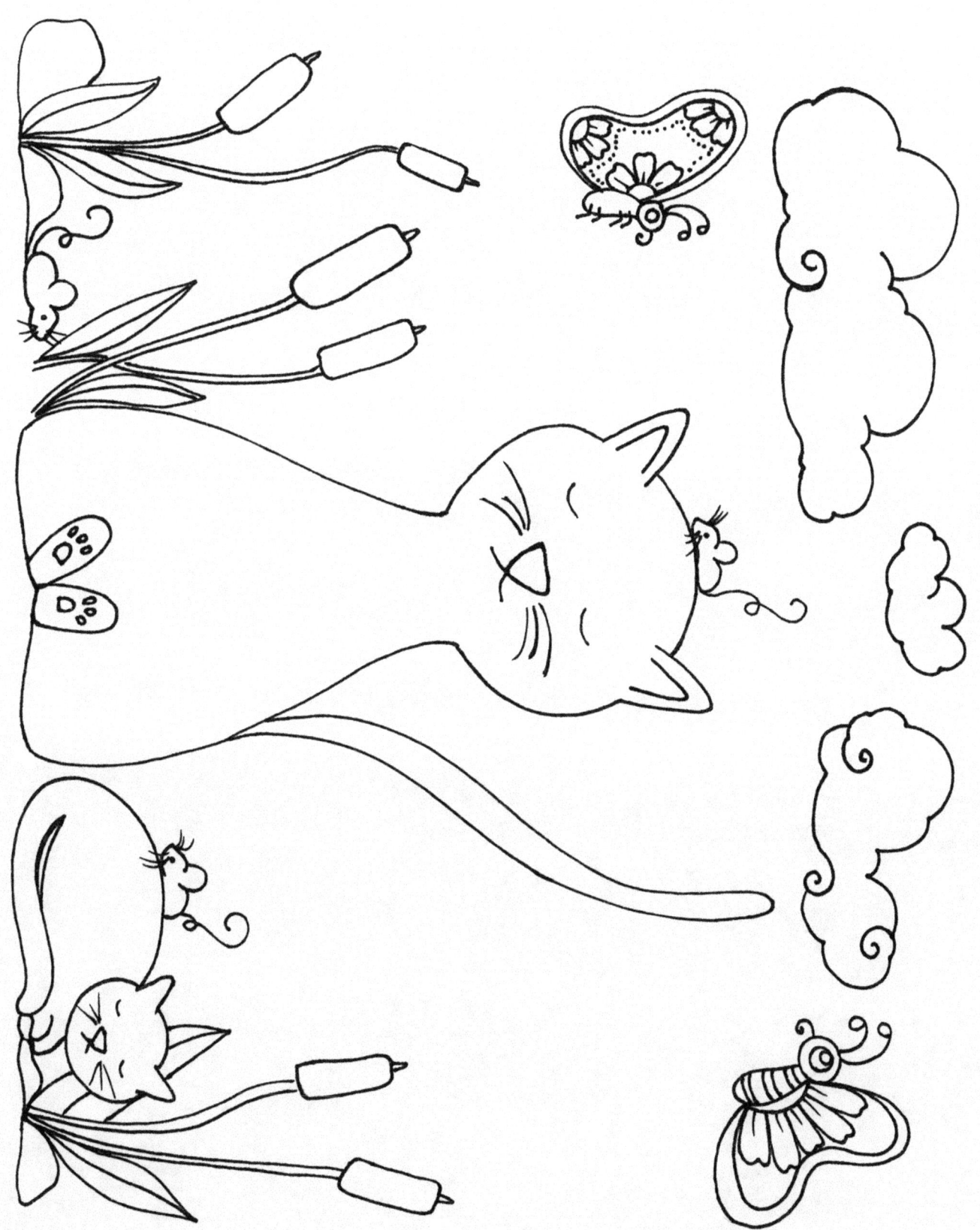

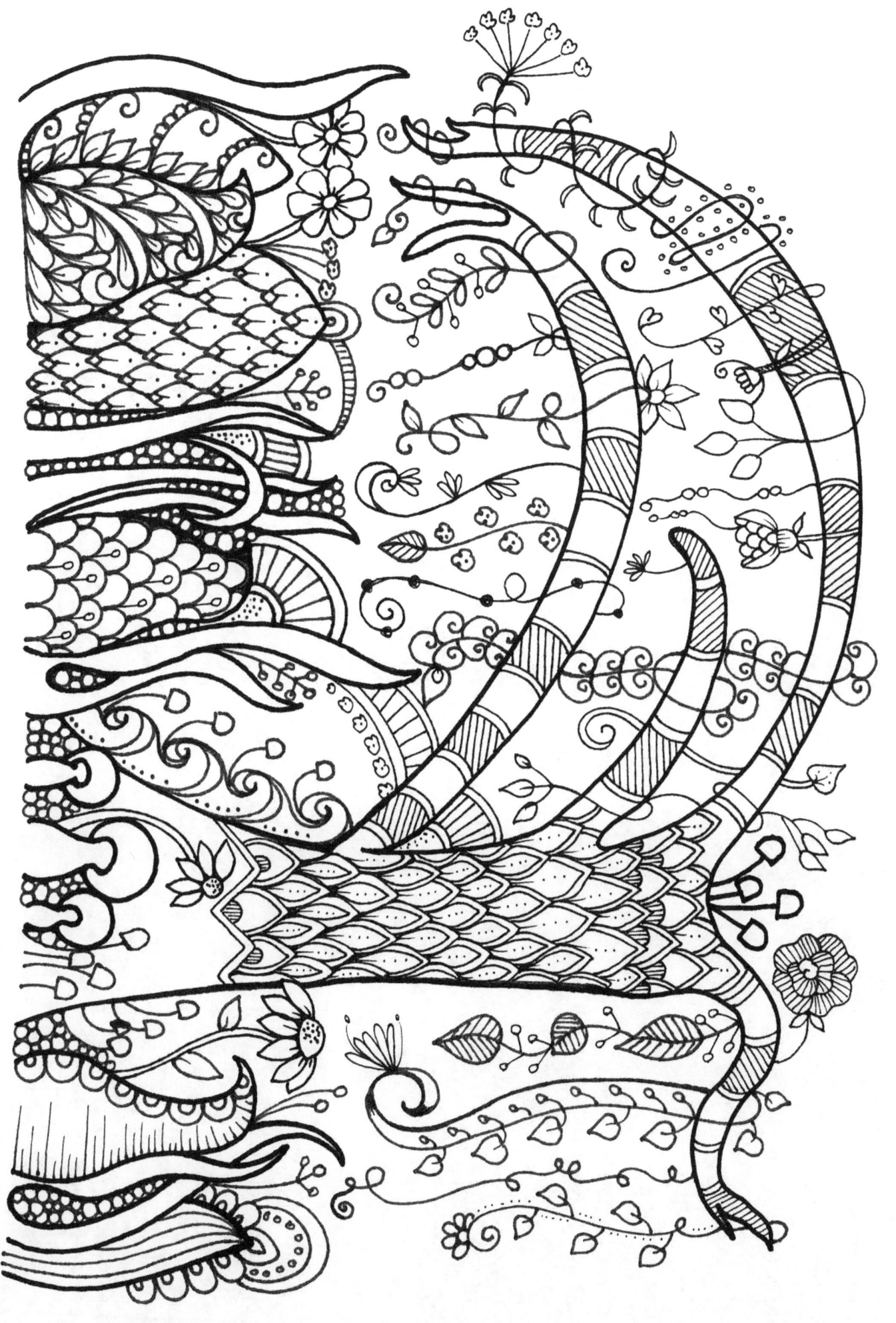

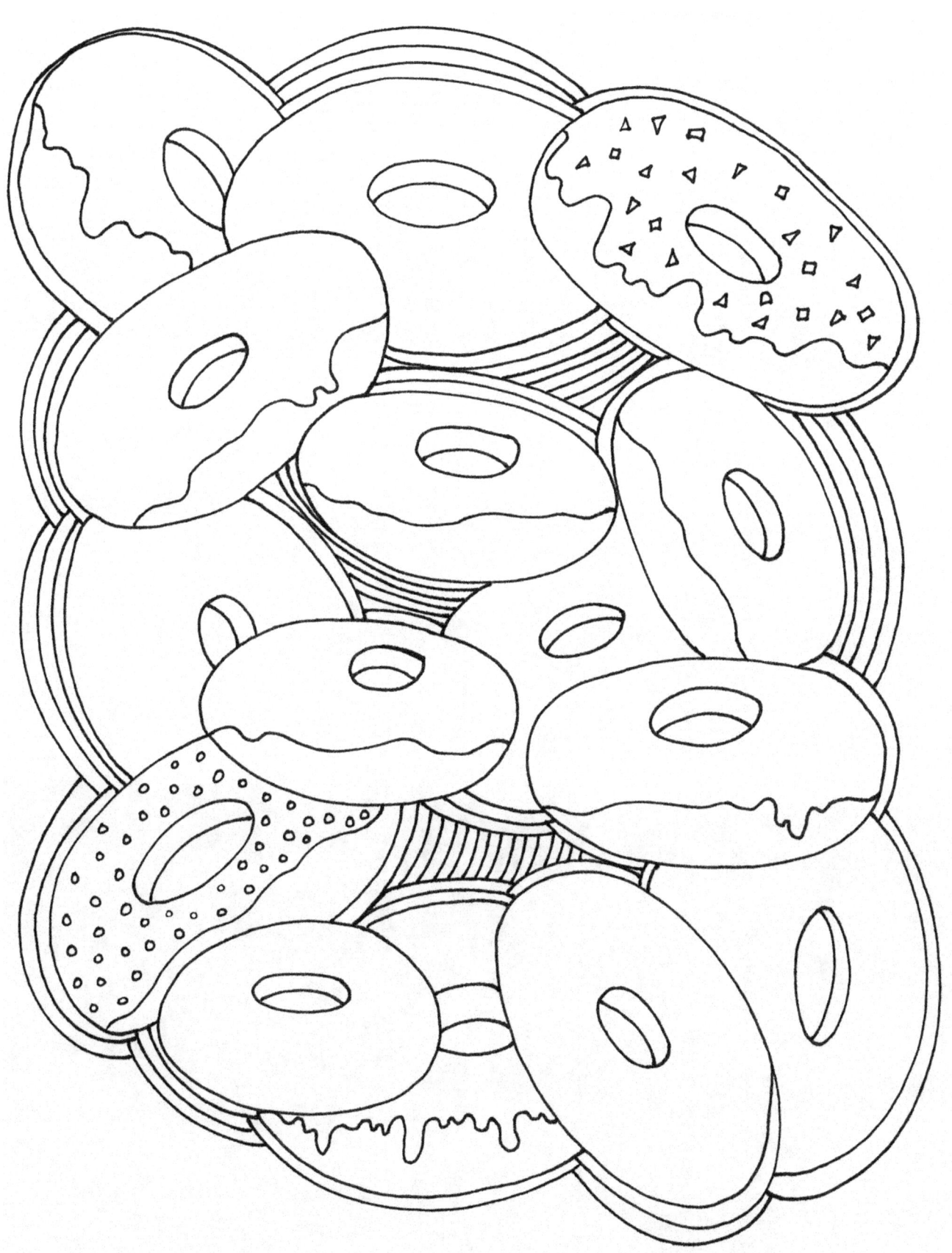

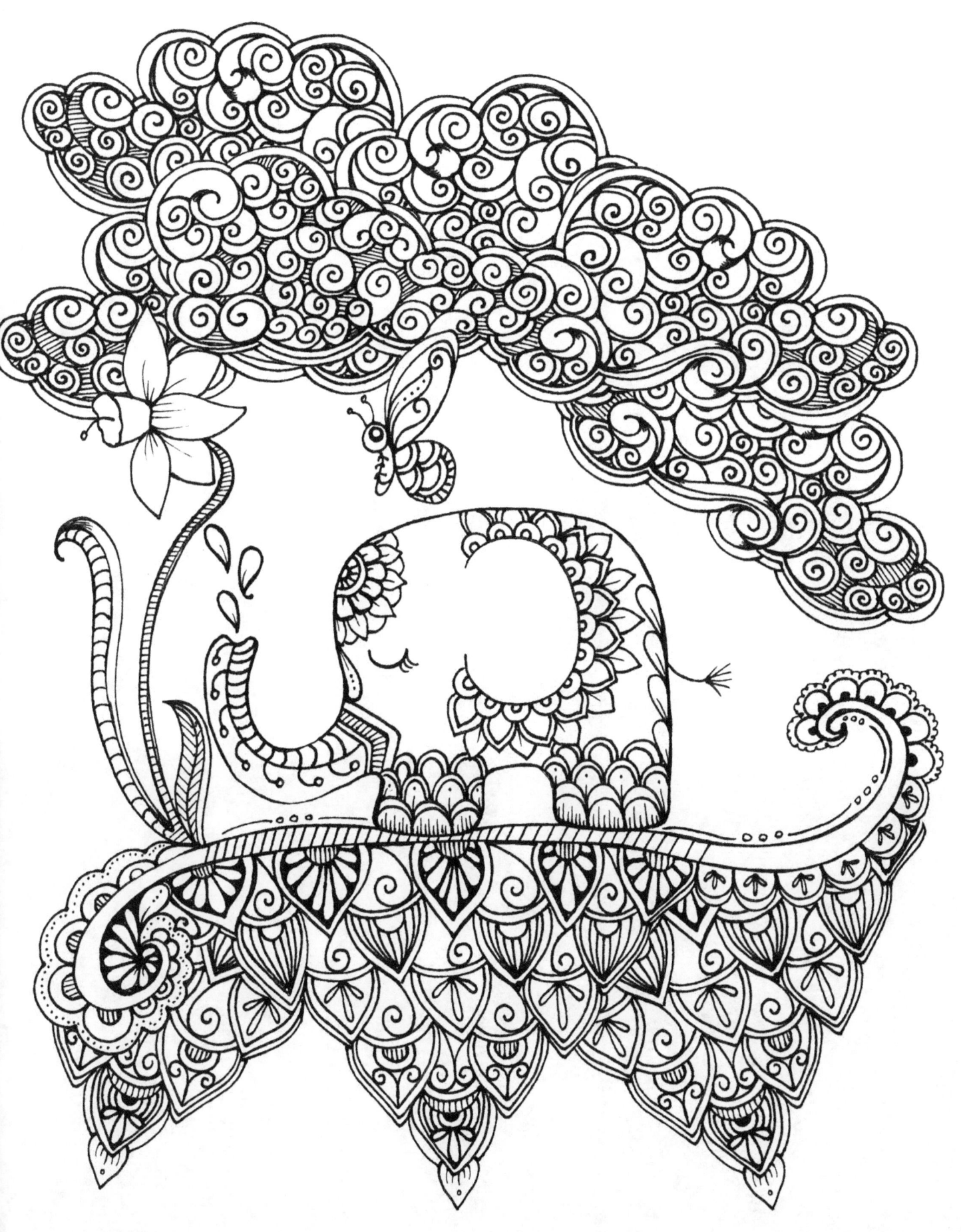

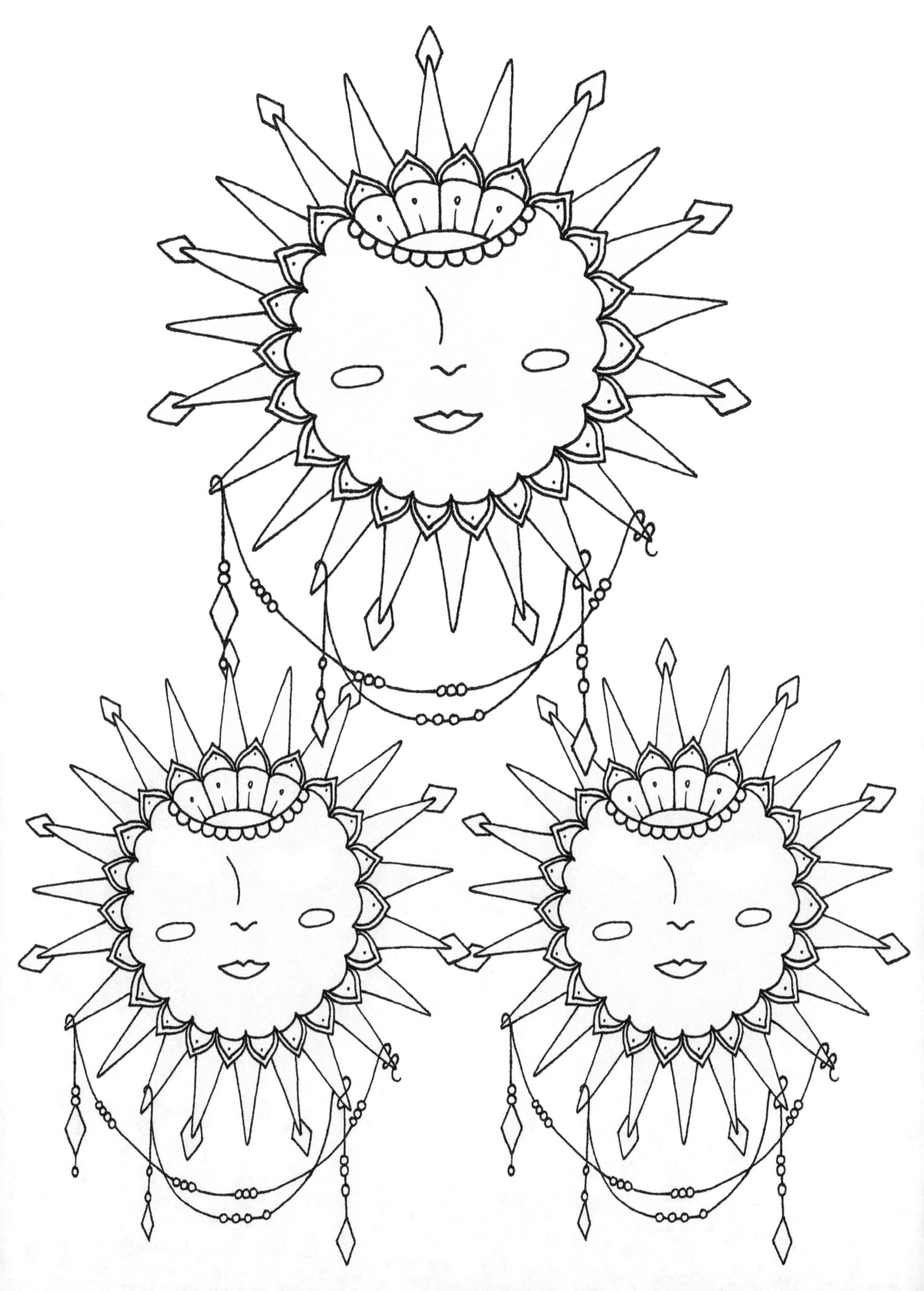

www.ingramcontent.com/pod-product-compliance
Lightning Source LLC
Chambersburg PA
CBHW080618190526
45169CB00009B/3229